Anytime
Casseroles

D0954361

Jean Paré

www.companyscoming.com
visit our website

Front Cover

1. Seafood Paella, page 85

Back Cover

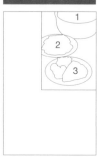

1. Corned Beef Casserole, page 32
2. Steak and Onion Pot Pie, page 30
3. Veggie Meatloaf Pie, page 34

Anytime Casseroles

Copyright © Company's Coming Publishing Limited

Third Printing April 2011

Library and Archives Canada Cataloguing in Publication
Paré, Jean, date-
Anytime casseroles / Jean Paré.
(Original series) Includes index.
At head of title: Company's Coming.
ISBN 978-1-897477-52-6
1. Casserole cookery. I. Title. II. Title: Company's Coming anytime casseroles. III. Series.
TX693.P363 2011   641.8'21   C2010-903737-5

Published by
Company's Coming Publishing Limited
2311 – 96 Street
Edmonton, Alberta, Canada T6N 1G3
Tel: 780-450-6223   Fax: 780-450-1857
www.companyscoming.com

Company's Coming is a registered trademark owned by Company's Coming Publishing Limited

We acknowledge the financial support of the Government of Canada through the Canada Book Fund for our publishing activities.

Printed in China

We gratefully acknowledge the following suppliers for their generous support of our Test and Photography Kitchens:

Broil King Barbecues
Corelle®
Hamilton Beach® Canada
Lagostina®
Proctor Silex® Canada
Tupperware®

Our special thanks to the following business for providing props for photography:

Stokes

Get more great recipes...FREE!

click

search

print

cook

From apple pie to zucchini bread, we've got you covered. Browse our free online recipes for Guaranteed Great!™ results.

You can also sign up to receive our **FREE online newsletter**. You'll receive exclusive offers, FREE recipes & cooking tips, new title previews, and much more...all delivered to your in-box.

So don't delay, visit our website today!

www.companyscoming.com
visit our ↑ website

Company's Coming Cookbooks

Quick & easy recipes; everyday ingredients!

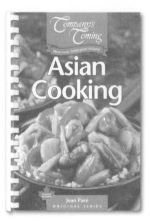

Original Series

- Softcover, 160 pages
- Lay-flat plastic comb binding
- Full-colour photos
- Nutrition information

Original Series

- Softcover, 160 pages
- Lay-flat plastic comb binding
- Full-colour photos
- Nutrition information

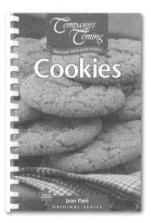

2-in-1 Cookbook Collection

- Softcover, 256 pages
- Lay-flat plastic coil binding
- Full-colour photos
- Nutrition information

Original Series

- Softcover, 160 pages
- Lay-flat plastic comb binding
- Full-colour photos
- Updated format

For a complete listing of our cookbooks, visit our website:
www.companyscoming.com

Table of Contents

Appetizers

Beef

Fish & Seafood

Vegetarian

Sides

Desserts

The Company's Coming Story

Jean Paré (pronounced "jeen PAIR-ee") grew up understanding that the combination of family, friends and home cooking is the best recipe for a good life. From her mother, she learned to appreciate good cooking, while her father praised even her earliest attempts in the kitchen. When Jean left home, she took with her a love of cooking, many family recipes and an intriguing desire to read cookbooks as if they were novels!

"Never share a recipe you wouldn't use yourself."

When her four children had all reached school age, Jean volunteered to cater the 50th anniversary celebration of the Vermilion School of Agriculture, now Lakeland College, in Alberta, Canada. Working out of her home, Jean prepared a dinner for more than 1,000 people, launching a flourishing catering operation that continued for over 18 years. During that time, she had countless opportunities to test new ideas with immediate feedback—resulting in empty plates and contented customers! Whether preparing cocktail sandwiches for a house party or serving a hot meal for 1,500 people, Jean Paré earned a reputation for great food, courteous service and reasonable prices.

As requests for her recipes increased, Jean was often asked the question, "Why don't you write a cookbook?" Jean responded by teaming up with her son, Grant Lovig, in the fall of 1980 to form Company's Coming Publishing Limited. The publication of *150 Delicious Squares* on April 14, 1981 marked the debut of what would soon become one of the world's most popular cookbook series.

The company has grown since those early days when Jean worked from a spare bedroom in her home. Today, she continues to write recipes while working closely with the staff of the Recipe Factory, as the Company's Coming test kitchen is affectionately known.

There she fills the role of mentor, assisting with the development of recipes people most want to use for everyday cooking and easy entertaining. Every Company's Coming recipe is *kitchen-tested* before it is approved for publication.

Jean's daughter, Gail Lovig, is responsible for marketing and distribution, leading a team that includes sales personnel located in major cities across Canada. Company's Coming cookbooks are distributed in Canada, the United States, Australia and other world markets. Bestsellers many times over in English, Company's Coming cookbooks have also been published in French and Spanish.

Familiar and trusted in home kitchens around the world, Company's Coming cookbooks are offered in a variety of formats. Highly regarded as kitchen workbooks, the softcover Original Series, with its lay-flat plastic comb binding, is still a favourite among readers.

Jean Paré's approach to cooking has always called for *quick and easy recipes* using *everyday ingredients*. That view has served her well. The recipient of many awards, including the Queen Elizabeth Golden Jubilee Medal, Jean was appointed Member of the Order of Canada, her country's highest lifetime achievement honour.

Jean continues to gain new supporters by adhering to what she calls The Golden Rule of Cooking: *Never share a recipe you wouldn't use yourself.* It's an approach that has worked—*millions of times over!*

Foreword

Winter weather always brings longings for comfort food, and casseroles hold those warm and cozy associations for many people. Casseroles are known for being family-friendly fare, and are often among the first foods that children really enjoy eating, causing many people to have fond childhood memories of their mother's tuna casserole or baked macaroni and cheese.

Not only are casseroles among the ultimate comfort foods—they're also known for their convenience. Casseroles often include many or all the components of a complete meal in one dish. Modern casserole dishes are also quite attractive—making it possible to prepare and serve your meal from a single dish. In addition to being a great way to use up leftovers, casseroles also make great leftovers! Many casseroles can be made in big batches and frozen, giving you easy options for future meals.

When we were planning *Anytime Casseroles*, we wanted to put together a collection of recipes that capture the homey feeling that most people associate with casseroles, while still providing a selection of chic, modern recipes that would be suitable for entertaining or for the more adventurous palate. We also wanted to provide recipes that would challenge the preconceived notions of casseroles. You'll find recipes for all sorts of dishes, from appetizers to main courses, sides, breakfasts and desserts. Your family will love our modernized version of the traditional

Tuna Casserole, and Bavarian Lasagna is a fun fusion of cultural cuisines that's sure to impress. Having friends over for a casual evening of entertaining is easy with our Baked Hot Pepper Nachos, and the Huevos Rancheros Casserole will inject a little flavour and fun into ordinary breakfast fare. The delightful Peachberry Clafouti is sure to add a touch of class to any event, without adding extra fuss.

Anytime Casseroles captures the traditional favourites you've come to love and provides you with unique and modern ideas that are guaranteed to become new additions to your recipe repertoire! You'll find no shortage of comfort food here, and the whole family is sure to appreciate adding a little new life to your casserole creations.

Jean Paré

Nutrition Information Guidelines

Each recipe is analyzed using the most current versions of the Canadian Nutrient File from Health Canada, and the United States Department of Agriculture (USDA) Nutrient Database for Standard Reference.

- If more than one ingredient is listed (such as "butter or hard margarine"), or if a range is given (1 – 2 tsp., 5 – 10 mL), only the first ingredient or first amount is analyzed.

- For meat, poultry and fish, the recommended serving size per person is 4 oz. (113 g) uncooked weight (without bone), which is 2 – 3 oz. (57 – 85 g) cooked weight (without bone)—approximately the size of a deck of playing cards.

- Milk used is 1% M.F. (milk fat), unless otherwise stated.

- Cooking oil used is canola oil, unless otherwise stated.

- Ingredients indicating "sprinkle," "optional," or "for garnish" are not included in the nutrition information.

- The fat in recipes and combination foods can vary greatly depending upon the sources and types of fats used in each specific ingredient. For these reasons, the amount of saturated, monounsaturated and polyunsaturated fats may not add up to the total fat content.

Comprehending Casseroles

A casserole, by definition, could be either of two things. "Casserole" originally referred to a covered baking dish, generally made of earthenware or glass. Over time, the word has also come to refer to the food cooked in a casserole dish. Most people think of casseroles as a savoury dish; however, sweet varieties are also common. Just think of cobblers and crisps!

History

As far as culinary history goes, the casserole is a relatively new invention. The first known casserole recipe in an English cookbook appeared in the early 1700s, though no one is quite sure when, or by whom, the first casserole was created. Originally, the casserole was a rather simple mix of rice and meat. Over time, casseroles have evolved and taken on different forms, with the notion of casseroles as a one-dish meal becoming common in the 1900s. Casseroles were widely popularized in the 1950s when new forms of bakeware were introduced. Today, they continue to be a popular and convenient method for preparing a complete meal.

Construction

When many people consider casseroles, they often think of canned soups, starchy ingredients, frozen vegetables and some form of meat. The traditional image often associated with this cooking method is actually quite limiting! It's true that casseroles may include some of these ingredients, but it is definitely not the rule. The truth is, the quality of the ingredients you use will be reflected in the taste of the finished dish. Keep this in mind when you consider adding suspicious-looking leftovers from the back of the fridge! Today's casseroles can actually include a wide range of ingredients, with bright flavours suited to any occasion.

The typical casserole generally consists of four basic components. Meat (or some other form of protein) and vegetables are common to almost all casseroles. You'll also need some sort of starchy binder—this often comes in the form of potatoes, pasta or rice. Lastly, you'll need to add liquid to cook these components. Stock, wine, soups or sauces are commonly used for this task. Some casseroles may also include other components, such as a crunchy topping or melted cheese. The combination of all these components generally results in a well-balanced meal, all cooked and served in the same dish!

Casseroles can also be a great way to use up leftovers. Leftover roast beef or turkey can easily be used, as can leftover steamed veggies, cooked pasta, mashed potatoes or rice. However, this doesn't give you free reign to empty your refrigerator into a casserole dish! Try to pair flavours that will work well together and always try to use up leftovers within a couple of days for best flavour and food safety.

Strategic Baking

First and foremost, using the correct bakeware is integral to making a successful casserole. Using the wrong size of dish can have disastrous results! Dishes that are too large can cause too much moisture to evaporate, while dishes that are too small could allow moisture to bubble up and flow over the sides of the dish! Dishes that are very shallow may cause food to cook too quickly, and those that are too deep may require longer bake times to reach safe temperatures. Use the casserole size or dimensions listed in the recipe as your guide—this is how we tested the recipe and the times or directions given will lead to casserole perfection!

It may be tempting to lift the lid and peek at your casserole creation as it cooks. Each time you do this, valuable heat and steam escape and your food will take longer to cook. You also run the risk of drying out your food as you lose moisture. This is why it is important to follow the directions outlined in the recipe. If the recipe asks you to bake the casserole with or without a lid, or if it asks you to stir at certain intervals, these instructions will impact the end result of your meal! Following the correct baking temperature is also important for success.

Remember that if you've used any raw meat, uncooked vegetables, rice, potatoes or pasta in your casserole, you will need to ensure that these elements are properly cooked before serving. Be sure to follow the doneness descriptors outlined in each recipe carefully. If you're reheating a casserole that you've already cooked, check the internal temperature before serving by inserting a meat thermometer into the centre of your casserole. If the temperature has reached at least 165°F (74°C), your casserole is safe to eat.

Casseroles that have been frozen can take longer to cook if you don't first thaw them. Cooking from frozen is something that should be done very carefully. Increasing the cooking temperature by a large amount can impact the end result greatly. For best results, allow casseroles that have been frozen to thaw in the refrigerator overnight.

Storage Suggestions

Many casseroles can be frozen for convenient future meals. We have indicated which recipes freeze and reheat particularly well. Casseroles can generally keep in the freezer for up to three months. When you're packing up your casseroles for the freezer, try to cover them tightly so that no air gets in. Many modern casserole dishes come with tight-fitting plastic lids that make them perfect for the freezer.

Crab Dip

A rich and cheesy dip with a nice lemony accent—great for serving with crackers and celery sticks. It makes a perfect little portion to serve with a spread of appetizers. You can make this a day ahead and chill, covered, until ready to bake.

Can of crabmeat, drained, cartilage removed, flaked	6 oz.	170 g
Block cream cheese, softened	4 oz.	125 g
Grated medium Cheddar cheese	1/2 cup	125 mL
Mayonnaise	1/2 cup	125 mL
Finely chopped seeded tomato	1/4 cup	60 mL
Finely chopped yellow pepper	1/4 cup	60 mL
Thinly sliced green onion	2 tbsp.	30 mL
Dijon mustard	1 tsp.	5 mL
Lemon juice	1 tsp.	5 mL
Worcestershire sauce	1/4 tsp.	1 mL
Hot pepper sauce	1/8 tsp.	0.5 mL
Paprika	1/8 tsp.	0.5 mL

Combine first 11 ingredients in medium bowl. Spread in greased 1 quart (1 L) casserole.

Sprinkle with paprika. Bake, uncovered, in 350°F (175°C) oven for about 35 minutes until bubbling and golden. Makes about 2 1/2 cups (625 mL).

1/4 cup (60 mL): 150 Calories; 14.0 g Total Fat (0 g Mono, 0 g Poly, 4.5 g Sat); 35 mg Cholesterol; 1 g Carbohydrate; 0 g Fibre; 5 g Protein; 230 mg Sodium

Paré Pointer
You can tell when trees have been scared to death.
They become petrified.

Appetizers

Spicy Porcupine Meatballs

That's one spicy meatball! Small porcupine meatballs are made with spicy Italian sausage and rice, with a nice herb sprinkle for colour. This recipe doubles well for larger gatherings, just make sure to up the size of your casserole dish.

Large egg, fork-beaten	1	1
Long-grain white rice	1/4 cup	60 mL
Finely chopped onion	2 tbsp.	30 mL
Dried basil	1/2 tsp.	2 mL
Garlic powder	1/2 tsp.	2 mL
Dried oregano	1/4 tsp.	1 mL
Pepper	1/4 tsp.	1 mL
Hot Italian sausage, casing removed	1/2 lb.	225 g
Lean ground beef	1/2 lb.	225 g
Can of diced tomatoes (with juice)	14 oz.	398 mL
Tomato sauce	1/2 cup	125 mL
Water	1/2 cup	125 mL
Dried crushed chilies	1/8 tsp.	0.5 mL
Chopped fresh parsley	2 tbsp.	30 mL

Combine first 7 ingredients in large bowl.

Add sausage and beef. Mix well. Roll into balls, using 1 tbsp. (15 mL) for each. Arrange in greased shallow 2 quart (2 L) casserole. Makes about 25 meatballs.

Combine next 4 ingredients in small bowl. Pour over meatballs. Cook, covered, in 375°F (190°C) oven for about 45 minutes until rice is tender and meatballs are no longer pink inside. Let stand, covered, for 10 minutes.

Sprinkle with parsley. Makes about 6 cups (1.5 L).

1/2 cup (125 mL): 140 Calories; 8.0 g Total Fat (1.5 g Mono, 0 g Poly, 3.0 g Sat); 35 mg Cholesterol; 6 g Carbohydrate; 0 g Fibre; 8 g Protein; 350 mg Sodium

Baked Tomato Basil Ricotta

Ricotta and tomato meld to create the perfect topping for toasted baguette slices or melba toast. This satisfying appetizer can be made a day ahead—just cover and chill until you're ready to bake.

Large eggs, fork-beaten	2	2
Ricotta cheese	2 cups	500 mL
Grated Parmesan cheese	3 tbsp.	50 mL
Chopped fresh basil	2 tsp.	10 mL
(or 1/2 tsp., 2 mL, dried)		
Sun-dried tomato pesto	2 tsp.	10 mL
Cooking oil	1 tsp.	5 mL
Coarsely ground pepper	1/8 tsp.	0.5 mL

Combine all 7 ingredients in medium bowl. Spread in greased 9 inch (23 cm) deep dish pie plate. Bake in 350°F (175°C) oven for about 35 minutes until set and golden. Makes about 2 1/2 cups (625 mL).

1/4 cup (60 mL): 110 Calories; 8.0 g Total Fat (2.5 g Mono, 0.5 g Poly, 4.5 g Sat); 50 mg Cholesterol; 2 g Carbohydrate; 0 g Fibre; 7 g Protein; 80 mg Sodium

Pesto Pizza Strips

Appealing pizza strips with pesto, veggies and lots of cheese. This fun and casual snack, served right from the pan, will be enjoyed by guests of all ages.

Frozen white bread dough, covered, thawed in refrigerator overnight	1	1
Basil pesto	2 tbsp.	30 mL
Thinly sliced fresh white mushrooms	1/2 cup	125 mL
Thinly sliced green pepper	1/4 cup	60 mL
Thinly sliced red onion	1/4 cup	60 mL
Grated mozzarella cheese	3/4 cup	175 mL
Grated Parmesan cheese	2 tbsp.	30 mL

Place dough in greased 9 x 13 inch (23 x 33 cm) pan. Pat out dough to edges of pan. Cover with greased waxed paper and tea towel. Let stand in oven with light on and door closed for about 30 minutes until slightly risen.

(continued on next page)

Appetizers

Brush pesto over dough. Scatter next 3 ingredients over top.

Sprinkle with mozzarella and Parmesan cheese. Bake in 400°F (205°C) oven for about 20 minutes until cheese is melted and edges are golden. Let stand for 5 minutes. Cut in half lengthwise. Cut each half into 6 strips. Makes 12 pizza strips.

1 pizza strip: 131 Calories; 3.5 g Total Fat (0 g Mono, 0 g Poly, 1.0 g Sat); 5 mg Cholesterol; 20 g Carbohydrate; trace Fibre; 5 g Protein; 273 mg Sodium

Honey Garlic Spareribs

Everyone will love to gather 'round a big pan of delicious spareribs—the glaze has just the right amount of chili spice and honey garlic flavour.

Sweet-and-sour-cut pork ribs, trimmed of fat and cut into 1-bone portions	3 lbs.	1.4 kg
Salt	1/2 tsp.	2 mL
Liquid honey	1/3 cup	75 mL
Soy sauce	3 tbsp.	50 mL
Dijon mustard	1 tbsp.	15 mL
Chili paste (sambal oelek)	1 tsp.	5 mL
Garlic powder	1 tsp.	5 mL
Sesame oil (for flavour)	1 tsp.	5 mL
Pepper	1/2 tsp.	2 mL

Place ribs in ungreased 9 x 13 inch (23 x 33 cm) pan. Sprinkle with salt. Toss. Cook, covered, in 350°F (175°C) oven for about 90 minutes until tender. Transfer with slotted spoon to large bowl. Discard drippings.

Combine remaining 7 ingredients in small bowl. Add to ribs. Stir until coated. Return to pan. Broil on top rack in oven for about 4 minutes, stirring once, until browned and glazed. Makes about 54 ribs.

1 rib: 38 Calories; 1.0 g Total Fat (0 g Mono, 0 g Poly, 0 g Sat); 10 mg Cholesterol; 2 g Carbohydrate; 0 g Fibre; 6 g Protein; 123 mg Sodium

Baked Hot Pepper Nachos

Everyone loves a big dish of nachos, and these have tasty jalapeños for just the right amount of heat. Use hotter chili peppers to crank it up a notch. Serve with salsa, guacamole and sour cream.

Cooking oil	1 tsp.	5 mL
Chopped onion	1 cup	250 mL
Chili powder	1 tsp.	5 mL
Ground cumin	1/2 tsp.	2 mL
Dried crushed chilies	1/4 tsp.	1 mL
Garlic powder	1/4 tsp.	1 mL
Chopped orange pepper	1 cup	250 mL
Chopped green pepper	1/2 cup	125 mL
Finely chopped fresh jalapeño pepper (see Tip, page 15)	1 tbsp.	15 mL
Bag of tortilla chips	11 1/4 oz.	320 g
Grated jalapeño Monterey Jack cheese	2 cups	500 mL
Chopped seeded tomato	1/2 cup	125 mL
Sliced green onion	1/4 cup	60 mL

Heat cooking oil in large frying pan on medium. Add next 5 ingredients. Cook for about 5 minutes, stirring often, until softened.

Add next 3 ingredients. Heat and stir for about 2 minutes until orange and green pepper start to soften.

Arrange half of chips in ungreased 9 x 13 inch (23 cm x 33 cm) baking dish. Scatter half of pepper mixture over top.

Sprinkle with half of cheese. Repeat with remaining chips, pepper mixture and cheese. Bake in 400°F (205°C) oven for about 10 minutes until cheese is melted.

Scatter tomato and green onion over top. Serves 8.

1 serving: 334 Calories; 20.0 g Total Fat (6.0 g Mono, 2.0 g Poly, 7.0 g Sat); 30 mg Cholesterol; 30 g Carbohydrate; 4 g Fibre; 10 g Protein; 408 mg Sodium

Pictured on page 17.

Appetizers

Peanut Red Curry Drumettes

These drumettes have a thick, spicy and peanutty sauce, with a peanut and cilantro garnish to round out the flavour. Serve this finger food with lots of napkins for sticky fingers!

Chicken drumettes	3 lbs.	1.4 kg
Sweet chili sauce	1/3 cup	75 mL
Peanut butter	1/4 cup	60 mL
Lime juice	3 tbsp.	50 mL
Thai red curry paste	1 tbsp.	15 mL
Finely grated ginger root	1 tsp.	5 mL
(or 1/4 tsp., 1 mL, ground ginger)		
Grated lime zest (see Tip, page 150)	1 tsp.	5 mL
Garlic clove, minced	1	1
(or 1/4 tsp., 1 mL, powder)		
Finely chopped salted peanuts	2 tbsp.	30 mL
Chopped fresh cilantro (or parsley)	2 tsp.	10 mL

Arrange drumettes in single layer in greased 9 x 13 inch (23 x 33 cm) pan. Broil on top rack in oven for about 15 minutes, turning at halftime, until browned. Transfer with slotted spoon to large bowl. Discard drippings.

Combine next 7 ingredients in small bowl. Add to drumettes. Stir until coated. Return to pan. Cook in 350°F (175°C) oven for about 45 minutes, turning at halftime, until chicken is no longer pink inside.

Sprinkle with peanuts and cilantro. Makes about 24 drumettes.

1 drumette: 150 Calories; 9.0 g Total Fat (3.0 g Mono, 1.5 g Poly, 2.5 g Sat); 50 mg Cholesterol; 3 g Carbohydrate; 0 g Fibre; 13 g Protein; 115 mg Sodium

Pictured on page 17.

 tip Hot peppers contain capsaicin in the seeds and ribs. Removing the seeds and ribs will reduce the heat. Wear rubber gloves when handling hot peppers and avoid touching your eyes. Wash your hands well afterwards.

Artichoke Bean Dip

Smooth, creamy beans and chunky artichokes make this tasty dip a great lower-fat alternative. Perfect for serving with pita chips or melba toast. Make this dip a day ahead and store it in the fridge until you're ready to bake.

Can of white kidney beans, rinsed and drained	19 oz.	540 mL
Sour cream	1/2 cup	125 mL
Reserved liquid from artichokes	1 tbsp.	15 mL
Sweet chili sauce	1 tbsp.	15 mL
Garlic clove, chopped (or 1/4 tsp., 1 mL, powder)	1	1
Salt	1/8 tsp.	0.5 mL
Jars of marinated artichoke hearts (6 oz., 170 mL, each), drained and liquid reserved, chopped	2	2
Finely chopped red pepper	1/4 cup	60 mL
Chopped fresh basil	2 tsp.	10 mL

Process first 6 ingredients in food processor until smooth. Transfer to medium bowl.

Add artichoke and red pepper. Stir. Spread in greased shallow 1 quart (1 L) casserole. Bake, uncovered, in 375°F (190°C) oven for about 30 minutes until heated through and golden. Stir.

Sprinkle with basil. Makes about 3 cups (750 mL).

1/4 cup (60 mL): 60 Calories; 3.0 g Total Fat (0 g Mono, 0 g Poly, 1.0 g Sat); 3 mg Cholesterol; 6 g Carbohydrate; trace Fibre; 3 g Protein; 115 mg Sodium

Pictured at right.

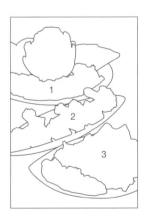

1. Artichoke Bean Dip, above
2. Peanut Red Curry Drumettes, page 15
3. Baked Hot Pepper Nachos, page 14

Apple Cheddar Raisin Toast

The classic combination of apples and cheese makes a tasty topper for baked raisin bread. This needs to chill overnight, so it's the perfect make-ahead option if you're expecting brunch guests.

Raisin bread slices	8	8
Chopped peeled tart apple (such as Granny Smith)	1 1/2 cups	375 mL
Large eggs	4	4
Milk	3/4 cup	175 mL
Granulated sugar	1 tbsp.	15 mL
Ground cinnamon	1/8 tsp.	0.5 mL
Salt	1/4 tsp.	1 mL
Pepper	1/8 tsp.	0.5 mL
Grated sharp Cheddar cheese	1 cup	250 mL

Arrange bread slices, slightly overlapping, in greased 9 x 13 inch (23 x 33 cm) baking dish. Scatter apple over top.

Whisk next 6 ingredients in medium bowl. Pour over top. Chill, covered, for at least 6 hours or overnight.

Sprinkle with cheese. Bake, uncovered, in 375°F (190°C) oven for about 40 minutes until set and edges of bread are crisp and golden. Serves 4.

1 serving: 360 Calories; 15.0 g Total Fat (3.0 g Mono, 1.0 g Poly, 7.0 g Sat); 170 mg Cholesterol; 40 g Carbohydrate; 3 g Fibre; 18 g Protein; 590 mg Sodium

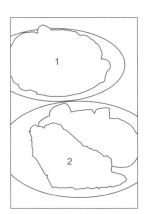

1. Raspberry French Toast, page 20
2. Oven Omelette, page 21

Raspberry French Toast

Prepare this beautiful French toast dish the night before and bake in the morning for hassle-free entertaining. The fresh raspberries scattered over top add a festive touch.

Large eggs	6	6
Milk	1 cup	250 mL
Vanilla extract	2 tsp.	10 mL
Ground cinnamon	1/2 tsp.	2 mL
Day-old French bread slices (1 inch, 2.5 cm, each)	12	12
TOPPING		
Seedless raspberry jam (not jelly)	1/3 cup	75 mL
Water	1/3 cup	75 mL
Granulated sugar	3 tbsp.	50 mL
Fresh (or frozen, thawed) raspberries	1 cup	250 mL

Whisk first 4 ingredients in large bowl.

Dip bread slices into egg mixture. Arrange, slightly overlapping, in well-greased 9 x 13 inch (23 x 33 cm) pan. Pour any remaining egg mixture over top. Chill, covered, for at least 6 hours or overnight. Bake, uncovered, in 375°F (190°C) oven for about 25 minutes until golden.

Topping: Stir first 3 ingredients in small saucepan on medium. Bring to a boil. Heat and stir for about 2 minutes until sugar is dissolved. Remove from heat. Let stand for 10 minutes to cool slightly. Drizzle over bread slices.

Scatter raspberries over top. Serves 6.

1 serving: 287 Calories; 6.0 g Total Fat (2.0 g Mono, 1.0 g Poly, 1.5 g Sat); 139 mg Cholesterol; 48 g Carbohydrate; 3 g Fibre; 11 g Protein; 360 mg Sodium

Pictured on page 18.

Variation: Make it extra special by adding 1 tbsp. (15 mL) orange-flavoured liqueur to the raspberry sauce.

Oven Omelette

A nice colourful omelette baked to golden perfection. The flavours of asparagus and potato are notable and delicious.

Diced peeled potato	1 cup	250 mL
Water	1 tbsp.	15 mL
Large eggs	8	8
Milk	1/2 cup	125 mL
Dried basil	1/2 tsp.	2 mL
Salt	1/4 tsp.	1 mL
Pepper	1/4 tsp.	1 mL
Chopped deli turkey breast slices	1/2 cup	125 mL
Chopped fresh asparagus	1/2 cup	125 mL
Chopped yellow pepper	1/2 cup	125 mL
Finely chopped onion	1/4 cup	60 mL
Grated havarti cheese	1 cup	250 mL

Put potato into medium microwave-safe bowl. Sprinkle with water. Microwave, covered, on high for about 5 minutes, stirring once, until tender (see Tip, below). Let stand, uncovered, for 5 minutes.

Whisk next 5 ingredients in large bowl.

Add next 4 ingredients and potato. Stir. Transfer to greased 9 x 13 inch (23 x 33 cm) baking dish.

Sprinkle with cheese. Bake in 400°F (205°C) oven for about 20 minutes until set. Cuts into 6 pieces.

1 piece: 170 Calories; 10.0 g Total Fat (2.0 g Mono, 1.0 g Poly, 4.5 g Sat); 200 mg Cholesterol; 8 g Carbohydrate; trace Fibre; 12 g Protein; 330 mg Sodium

Pictured on page 18.

 tip The microwaves used in our test kitchen are 900 watts—but microwaves are sold in many different powers. You should be able to find the wattage of yours by opening the door and looking for the mandatory label. If your microwave is more than 900 watts, you may need to reduce the cooking time. If it's less than 900 watts, you'll probably need to increase the cooking time.

Huevos Rancheros Casserole

A hearty and satisfying Mexican-style casserole that the whole family is sure to love! Loaded with eggs, corn and beans, all topped with a refreshing burst of colour from avocado and tomato.

Can of black beans, rinsed and drained	19 oz.	540 mL
Fresh (or frozen, thawed) kernel corn	1 cup	250 mL
Salsa	1 cup	250 mL
Large eggs	10	10
Finely chopped green onion	2 tbsp.	30 mL
Milk	2 tbsp.	30 mL
Salt	1/8 tsp.	0.5 mL
Grated medium Cheddar cheese	1 cup	250 mL
Chopped avocado	1/2 cup	125 mL
Chopped tomato	1/2 cup	125 mL
Crushed tortilla chips	1/4 cup	60 mL
Chopped fresh cilantro (or parsley)	2 tsp.	10 mL

Combine first 3 ingredients in greased shallow 2 quart (2 L) casserole.

Whisk next 4 ingredients in medium bowl. Pour over black bean mixture.

Sprinkle with cheese. Bake, uncovered, in 350°F (175°C) oven for about 50 minutes until set and golden.

Scatter remaining 4 ingredients, in order given, over top. Serve immediately. Serves 8.

1 serving: 250 Calories; 12.0 g Total Fat (3.5 g Mono, 1.0 g Poly, 4.5 g Sat); 185 mg Cholesterol; 23 g Carbohydrate; 6 g Fibre; 15 g Protein; 530 mg Sodium

Pictured on page 89.

Paré Pointer

When you stumble and hit the floor,
you get so angry you hit the ceiling.

Ham and Leek Cobbler

Delicious! Flavourful ham and leeks are accented by fragrant rosemary, all covered with a golden biscuit topping.

Cooking oil	2 tsp.	10 mL
Sliced leek (white part only)	4 cups	1 L
Finely chopped fennel bulb (white part only)	1 cup	250 mL
Dried rosemary, crushed	3/4 tsp.	4 mL
Pepper	1/4 tsp.	1 mL
Frozen peas	1 1/2 cups	375 mL
Chopped cooked ham	1 cup	250 mL
Prepared vegetable broth	1/4 cup	60 mL
Dijon mustard	1 tbsp.	15 mL
All-purpose flour	2/3 cup	150 mL
Quick-cooking rolled oats	1/3 cup	75 mL
Baking powder	2 tsp.	10 mL
Salt	1/4 tsp.	1 mL
Cold butter (or hard margarine), cut up	1/3 cup	75 mL
Large egg, fork-beaten	1	1
Buttermilk (or soured milk, see Tip, page 94)	2/3 cup	150 mL

Heat cooking oil in large frying pan on medium. Add next 4 ingredients. Cook for about 15 minutes, stirring occasionally, until leek is softened.

Add next 4 ingredients. Cook for about 5 minutes, stirring often, until heated through. Transfer to ungreased 8 x 8 inch (20 x 20 cm) baking dish.

Combine next 4 ingredients in medium bowl. Cut in butter until mixture resembles coarse crumbs.

Add egg and buttermilk. Stir until just moistened. Drop by mounded tablespoonfuls over hot leek mixture. Bake in 400°F (205°C) oven for about 30 minutes until golden and wooden pick inserted in centre of biscuit comes out clean. Serves 4.

1 serving: 430 Calories; 21.0 g Total Fat (6.0 g Mono, 2.5 g Poly, 11.0 g Sat); 95 mg Cholesterol; 45 g Carbohydrate; 7 g Fibre; 17 g Protein; 1080 mg Sodium

Baked Blueberry Pecan Oatmeal

A warm, comforting breakfast casserole that can be served with yogurt.
Blueberry adds sweetness while pecans add delectable crunch.

Quick-cooking rolled oats	2 cups	500 mL
Milk	1 1/4 cups	300 mL
Unsweetened applesauce	3/4 cup	175 mL
Dried blueberries (or cranberries)	1/2 cup	125 mL
Brown sugar, packed	1/4 cup	60 mL
Chopped pecans, toasted (see Tip, page 86)	1/4 cup	60 mL
Wheat germ	1/4 cup	60 mL
Butter (or hard margarine), melted	2 tbsp.	30 mL
Ground cinnamon	1 tsp.	5 mL
Vanilla extract	1 tsp.	5 mL
Ground ginger	1/2 tsp.	2 mL
Salt	1/2 tsp.	2 mL

Combine all 12 ingredients in medium bowl. Spread evenly in greased
8 x 8 inch (20 x 20 cm) baking dish. Bake, covered, in 350°F (175°C) oven
for about 20 minutes until liquid is absorbed. Serves 4.

1 serving: 460 Calories; 15.0 g Total Fat (5.0 g Mono, 2.5 g Poly, 5.0 g Sat); 18 mg Cholesterol;
72 g Carbohydrate; 10 g Fibre; 12 g Protein; 336 mg Sodium

Sausage Vegetable Hash

This hearty and welcoming casserole is packed with plenty of potatoes,
sausage and cheese.

Cooking oil	2 tsp.	10 mL
Diced unpeeled potato	4 cups	1 L
Chopped onion	2 cups	500 mL
Turkey breakfast sausage, casing removed	3/4 lb.	340 g
Diced red pepper	1 cup	250 mL
Dried basil	1 tsp.	5 mL
Salt	1/4 tsp.	1 mL
Pepper	1/4 tsp.	1 mL

(continued on next page)

| Grated mozzarella cheese | 1/2 cup | 125 mL |
| Sliced green onion | 1/4 cup | 60 mL |

Heat cooking oil in large frying pan on medium. Add next 3 ingredients. Scramble-fry for about 10 minutes until potato starts to soften.

Add next 4 ingredients. Heat and stir for 1 minute. Transfer to greased shallow 2 quart (2 L) casserole. Bake, uncovered, in 400°F (205°C) oven for about 30 minutes until potato is tender.

Sprinkle cheese and green onion over top. Bake, uncovered, for about 5 minutes until cheese is melted. Makes about 7 cups (1.75 L).

1 cup (250 mL): 180 Calories; 6.0 g Total Fat (0 g Mono, 1.0 g Poly, 2.0 g Sat); 25 mg Cholesterol; 23 g Carbohydrate; 2 g Fibre; 11 g Protein; 560 mg Sodium

---

Sausage Onion Quiche

A quiche packed with flavour—without the extra work of making a crust! Mildly spicy sausage and eggs are topped with cheese for a combination that's sure to become a breakfast or brunch favourite.

Hot Italian sausage, casing removed	1/2 lb.	225 g
Chopped onion	1 cup	250 mL
Large eggs	4	4
Milk	1 1/4 cups	300 mL
All-purpose flour	2 tbsp.	30 mL
Garlic powder	1/4 tsp.	1 mL
Pepper	1/4 tsp.	1 mL
Grated Italian cheese blend	1 cup	250 mL

Scramble-fry sausage and onion in large frying pan on medium for about 10 minutes until sausage is no longer pink. Drain.

Whisk next 5 ingredients in medium bowl.

Add cheese and sausage mixture. Stir. Transfer to greased 9 inch (23 cm) deep dish pie plate. Bake in 375°F (190°C) oven for about 45 minutes until knife inserted in centre comes out clean. Let stand on wire rack for 10 minutes. Cuts into 6 wedges.

1 wedge: 270 Calories; 17.0 g Total Fat (6.0 g Mono, 1.5 g Poly, 7.0 g Sat); 130 mg Cholesterol; 9 g Carbohydrate; 0 g Fibre; 18 g Protein; 680 mg Sodium

Tofu Scramble Wraps

Tasty tortilla wraps hold a nicely seasoned blend of scrambled tofu and veggies. This dish could easily fool any family members who are still resistant to trying tofu! For easy crumbling, cut the tofu into six or eight pieces first.

Cooking oil	2 tsp.	10 mL
Chopped fresh white mushrooms	1 cup	250 mL
Chopped onion	1 cup	250 mL
Chopped yellow pepper	1 cup	250 mL
Chopped zucchini (with peel)	1 cup	250 mL
Package of firm tofu, crumbled	12 oz.	350 g
Thinly sliced green onion	2 tbsp.	30 mL
Soy sauce	1 tbsp.	15 mL
Turmeric	1/2 tsp.	2 mL
Cayenne pepper	1/4 tsp.	1 mL
Garlic clove, minced	1	1
(or 1/4 tsp., 1 mL, powder)		
Ground cumin	1/4 tsp.	1 mL
Salt	1/2 tsp.	2 mL
Pepper	1/4 tsp.	1 mL
Flour tortillas (9 inch, 23 cm, diameter)	4	4

Heat cooking oil in large frying pan on medium. Add next 4 ingredients. Cook for about 10 minutes, stirring often, until onion is softened and liquid is evaporated.

Add next 9 ingredients. Cook for about 5 minutes, stirring occasionally, until heated through.

Spoon tofu mixture along centre of tortillas. Fold sides over filling. Roll up from bottom to enclose. Arrange, seam-side down, in greased 8 x 8 inch (20 x 20 cm) baking dish. Bake in 400°F (205°C) oven for about 15 minutes until golden. Makes 4 wraps.

1 wrap: 420 Calories; 15.0 g Total Fat (5.0 g Mono, 6.0 g Poly, 2.5 g Sat); 0 mg Cholesterol; 52 g Carbohydrate; 5 g Fibre; 22 g Protein; 830 mg Sodium

Croque Monsieur Bake

This make-ahead dish is approachable and crowd-pleasing—big, filling croque monsieur (pronounced KROHK muhs-YOOR) sandwiches make a delicious all-in-one brunch offering when filled with ham, Dijon and cheese.

Dijon mustard	3 tbsp.	50 mL
Finely chopped green onion	1 tbsp.	15 mL
Prepared horseradish	1 tsp.	5 mL
French bread slices (1/2 inch, 12 mm, each)	12	12
Grated Italian cheese blend	1 cup	250 mL
Deli ham slices (about 7 oz., 200 g), halved	6	6
Large eggs	8	8
Milk	1 1/2 cups	375 mL
Grated Italian cheese blend	1/2 cup	125 mL
Finely chopped red pepper	1/4 cup	60 mL

Combine first 3 ingredients in small bowl. Spread over 1 side of each bread slice.

Sprinkle half of first amount of cheese over mustard mixture on 6 bread slices. Place ham slices over top. Sprinkle with remaining cheese. Top with remaining bread slices, mustard mixture-side down. Arrange in greased 9 x 13 inch (23 x 33 cm) pan.

Whisk eggs and milk in medium bowl. Pour over sandwiches. Chill, covered, for at least 6 hours or overnight.

Sprinkle with second amount of cheese and red pepper. Bake, uncovered, in 350°F (175°C) oven for about 40 minutes until golden. Makes 6 sandwiches.

1 sandwich: 382 Calories; 15.0 g Total Fat (3.0 g Mono, 1.0 g Poly, 6.0 g Sat); 225 mg Cholesterol; 41 g Carbohydrate; 2 g Fibre; 27 g Protein; 1128 mg Sodium

Paré Pointer

Can you fire a weather forecaster for shooting the breeze?

Spanish Pot Roast

This pleasing pot roast is surrounded by veggies and olives to create a flavourful all-in-one meal! Leftover pot roast reheats best in the oven—just place it in a baking dish and pour the remaining sauce over top. Leftover veggies can be heated in the microwave.

Boneless beef cross-rib roast, trimmed of fat	3 lbs.	1.4 kg
Salt	1/2 tsp.	2 mL
Pepper	1/4 tsp.	1 mL
Cooking oil	1 tbsp.	15 mL
Prepared beef broth	1 1/2 cups	375 mL
All-purpose flour	1/3 cup	75 mL
Finely chopped onion	1/4 cup	60 mL
White wine vinegar	1/4 cup	60 mL
Granulated sugar	3 tbsp.	50 mL
Tomato paste (see Tip, page 111)	3 tbsp.	50 mL
Worcestershire sauce	1 tsp.	5 mL
Garlic clove, minced (or 1/4 tsp., 1 mL, powder)	1	1
Baby potatoes, larger ones halved	2 lbs.	900 g
Medium carrots, quartered lengthwise and cut into 2 inch (5 cm) pieces	6	6
Medium parsnips, quartered lengthwise and cut into 2 inch (5 cm) pieces (see Note)	3	3
Sliced green olives	1/2 cup	125 mL

Sprinkle roast with salt and pepper.

Heat cooking oil in large frying pan on medium-high. Add roast. Cook for about 10 minutes, turning occasionally, until browned on all sides. Place in large roasting pan. Reduce heat to medium.

Whisk next 8 ingredients in small bowl. Add to same frying pan. Heat and stir, scraping any brown bits from bottom of pan, until boiling. Pour over roast. Cook, covered, in 300°F (150°C) oven for 1 hour.

Place remaining 4 ingredients around roast. Stir until coated. Cook, covered, for about 90 minutes until roast and vegetables are tender. Serves 8.

(continued on next page)

Beef

1 serving: 620 Calories; 33.0 g Total Fat (14.0 g Mono, 2.5 g Poly, 12.0 g Sat); 110 mg Cholesterol; 42 g Carbohydrate; 4 g Fibre; 38 g Protein; 590 mg Sodium

Note: Parsnips can be quite thick at the top and taper to very thin at the bottom. Cut to uniform size for more even cooking.

Beef Hot Pot

A mildly spicy hot pot baked in a Dutch oven. A good dose of vegetables offer lots of colour and texture. Freeze leftovers in individual portions and reheat in the microwave for convenient last-minute meals.

Stewing beef, trimmed of fat	1 1/2 lbs.	680 g
Prepared beef broth	3 cups	750 mL
Sliced carrot	2 cups	500 mL
Sliced fresh shiitake mushrooms	2 cups	500 mL
Can of cut baby corn, drained	14 oz.	398 mL
Can of shoestring-style bamboo shoots, drained	8 oz.	227 mL
Chopped onion	1 cup	250 mL
Water	1 cup	250 mL
Finely grated ginger root (or 1/2 tsp., 2 mL, ground ginger)	2 tsp.	10 mL
Chili paste (sambal oelek)	1 tsp.	5 mL
Garlic clove, minced (or 1/4 tsp., 1 mL, powder)	1	1
Chopped fresh spinach leaves, lightly packed	1 cup	250 mL
Sliced trimmed sugar snap peas	1 cup	250 mL
Sliced green onion	3 tbsp.	50 mL
Rice vinegar	1 tbsp.	15 mL
Soy sauce	1 tbsp.	15 mL
Sesame oil (for flavour)	1 tsp.	5 mL
Salt	1/4 tsp.	1 mL

Combine first 11 ingredients in Dutch oven. Cook, covered, in 325°F (160°C) oven for about 2 1/2 hours until beef is tender. Remove from oven.

Add remaining 7 ingredients. Stir. Let stand, covered, for 10 minutes. Makes about 10 cups (2.5 L).

1 cup (250 mL): 170 Calories; 6.0 g Total Fat (2.0 g Mono, 0.5 g Poly, 2.0 g Sat); 35 mg Cholesterol; 12 g Carbohydrate; 2 g Fibre; 18 g Protein; 490 mg Sodium

Beef

29

Steak and Onion Pot Pie

This inviting, pastry-topped pot pie lives up to all expectations with its rich thyme gravy, tender beef and vegetables.

Cooking oil	2 tsp.	10 mL
Beef top sirloin steak, trimmed of fat and cut into 3/4 inch (2 cm) pieces	1 lb.	454 g
Montreal steak spice	1/4 tsp.	1 mL
Cooking oil	2 tsp.	10 mL
Chopped onion	2 cups	500 mL
Chopped peeled potato	1 1/2 cups	375 mL
Chopped carrot	1 cup	250 mL
All-purpose flour	3 tbsp.	50 mL
Dried thyme	1/2 tsp.	2 mL
Prepared beef broth	2 cups	500 mL
Package of puff pastry (14 oz., 397 g), thawed according to package directions	1/2	1/2
Large egg	1	1
Water	1 tbsp.	15 mL

Heat first amount of cooking oil in large frying pan on medium-high. Add beef. Sprinkle with steak spice. Cook for about 5 minutes, stirring occasionally, until browned. Transfer to greased 8 x 8 inch (20 x 20 cm) baking dish. Reduce heat to medium.

Heat second amount of cooking oil in same frying pan. Add next 3 ingredients. Cook for about 12 minutes, stirring often, until potato starts to soften and brown.

Add flour and thyme. Heat and stir for 1 minute. Slowly add broth, stirring constantly until smooth. Heat and stir until boiling and thickened. Spoon over beef.

Roll out puff pastry on lightly floured surface to 10 inch (25 cm) square.

Whisk egg and water in small bowl. Brush top rim of baking dish with egg mixture. Place pastry over beef mixture. Press pastry onto dish to seal. Brush with remaining egg mixture. Cut several small vents in top to allow steam to escape. Bake in 400°F (205°C) oven for about 25 minutes until pastry is puffed and golden. Serves 4.

(continued on next page)

Beef

1 serving: 660 Calories; 37.0 g Total Fat (18.0 g Mono, 6.0 g Poly, 11.0 g Sat); 80 mg Cholesterol; 48 g Carbohydrate; 3 g Fibre; 32 g Protein; 720 mg Sodium

Pictured on page 35 and on back cover.

Texas Chili

A little like stew and a lot like chili—this all-in-one dish will make chili night exciting again! Serve with garlic toast or whole-wheat buns and a fresh green salad to make a complete meal.

Cooking oil	2 tsp.	10 mL
Boneless beef blade (or chuck) roast, trimmed of fat and cut into 1/2 inch (12 mm) pieces	1 1/2 lbs.	680 g
Salt	1/4 tsp.	1 mL
Pepper	1/4 tsp.	1 mL
Prepared beef broth	1 1/2 cups	375 mL
Can of romano beans, rinsed and drained	19 oz.	540 mL
Diced peeled potato	2 cups	500 mL
Can of diced tomatoes (with juice)	14 oz.	398 mL
Chopped celery	1 1/2 cups	375 mL
Chopped onion	1 1/2 cups	375 mL
Frozen kernel corn	1 cup	250 mL
Bacon slices, cooked crisp and crumbled	4	4
Chili powder	2 tbsp.	30 mL
Brown sugar, packed	1 tbsp.	15 mL
Cocoa, sifted if lumpy	1 tbsp.	15 mL
Tomato paste (see Tip, page 111)	1 tbsp.	15 mL

Heat cooking oil in Dutch oven on medium-high. Add beef. Sprinkle with salt and pepper. Cook for about 10 minutes, stirring occasionally, until browned.

Add broth. Heat and stir, scraping any brown bits from bottom of pan, until boiling.

Add remaining 11 ingredients. Stir. Cook, covered, in 350°F (175°C) oven for about 90 minutes until beef and vegetables are tender. Makes about 9 cups (2.25 L).

1 cup (250 mL): 217 Calories; 7.0 g Total Fat (3.0 g Mono, 1.0 g Poly, 2.5 g Sat); 44 mg Cholesterol; 19 g Carbohydrate; 3 g Fibre; 19 g Protein; 589 mg Sodium

Corned Beef Casserole

What's the secret to this tasty casserole? Packing a hearty dose of veggies into the classic combination of corned beef and cabbage. A nice Dijon speckle adds a complementary mustard flavour.

Cooking oil	1 tsp.	5 mL
Shredded cabbage, lightly packed	4 cups	1 L
Chopped carrot	2 cups	500 mL
Sliced onion	2 cups	500 mL
Pepper	1/4 tsp.	1 mL
Water	1/4 cup	60 mL
Water	8 cups	2 L
Salt	1 tsp.	5 mL
Broad egg noodles	4 cups	1 L
Deli corned beef, cut into 1/2 inch (12 mm) strips	3/4 lb.	340 g
Alfredo pasta sauce	1 cup	250 mL
Water	1/2 cup	125 mL
Chopped fresh parsley (or 2 tsp., 10 mL, flakes)	1/4 cup	60 mL
Dijon mustard (with whole seeds)	2 tbsp.	30 mL

Heat cooking oil in large frying pan on medium-high. Add next 4 ingredients. Stir. Add first amount of water. Cook for about 8 minutes, stirring occasionally, until onion starts to brown.

Combine second amount of water and salt in Dutch oven. Bring to a boil. Add noodles. Boil, uncovered, for about 6 minutes, stirring occasionally, until tender but firm. Drain. Return to same pot.

Add remaining 5 ingredients and cabbage mixture. Stir. Transfer to greased 3 quart (3 L) casserole. Bake, covered, in 375°F (190°C) oven for about 40 minutes until heated through. Makes about 9 cups (2.25 L).

1 cup (250 mL): 210 Calories; 7.0 g Total Fat (0 g Mono, 0.5 g Poly, 4.0 g Sat); 50 mg Cholesterol; 22 g Carbohydrate; 2 g Fibre; 12 g Protein; 590 mg Sodium

Pictured on page 35 and on back cover.

Black Bean Shepherd's Pie

Creamy golden potato tops tender beef and vegetables in this all-in-one casserole. Corn and black beans add a bit of Tex-Mex flavour that the kids will love.

Chopped peeled potato	5 cups	1.25 L
Grated sharp Cheddar cheese	1 cup	250 mL
Milk	1/4 cup	60 mL
Butter (or hard margarine)	1 tbsp.	15 mL
Cooking oil	1 tsp.	5 mL
Lean ground beef	1 lb.	454 g
Chopped fresh white mushrooms	1 cup	250 mL
Chopped onion	1 cup	250 mL
Finely chopped carrot	1/2 cup	125 mL
Salt	1/2 tsp.	2 mL
Pepper	1/4 tsp.	1 mL
Can of black beans, rinsed and drained	19 oz.	540 mL
Can of diced tomatoes (with juice)	14 oz.	398 mL
Chopped red pepper	1 cup	250 mL
Frozen kernel corn	1 cup	250 mL
Ketchup	2 tbsp.	30 mL
All-purpose flour	1 tbsp.	15 mL

Pour water into large saucepan until about 1 inch (2.5 cm) deep. Add potato. Cover. Bring to a boil. Reduce heat to medium. Boil gently for 12 to 15 minutes until tender. Drain. Return to same pot. Mash.

Add next 3 ingredients. Mash. Cover to keep warm.

Heat cooking oil in large frying pan on medium. Add next 6 ingredients. Scramble-fry for about 10 minutes until beef is no longer pink.

Add remaining 6 ingredients. Stir. Transfer to ungreased 9 x 13 inch (23 x 33 cm) baking dish. Spread potato mixture evenly over top. Bake in 375°F (190°C) oven for about 40 minutes until heated through and bubbling at edges. Serves 8.

1 serving: 400 Calories; 15.0 g Total Fat (4.0 g Mono, 1.0 g Poly, 7.0 g Sat); 55 mg Cholesterol; 40 g Carbohydrate; 7 g Fibre; 23 g Protein; 600 mg Sodium

Veggie Meatloaf Pie

These thick meatloaf wedges are fortified with veggie goodness and topped with a deliciously sweet ketchup glaze—sure to be an instant favourite with the kids! Great served with mashed potatoes.

Large eggs, fork-beaten	2	2
Frozen pea and carrot mix, thawed	1 1/2 cups	375 mL
Frozen kernel corn, thawed	3/4 cup	175 mL
Box of cornbread stovetop stuffing mix	4 1/2 oz.	120 g
Ketchup	2 tbsp.	30 mL
Montreal steak spice	1/2 tsp.	2 mL
Lean ground beef	1 1/2 lbs.	680 g
Ketchup	1/4 cup	60 mL

Combine first 6 ingredients in large bowl.

Add beef. Mix well. Press into greased 9 inch (23 cm) deep dish pie plate.

Spread second amount of ketchup over top. Cook in 350°F (175°C) oven for about 55 minutes until internal temperature reaches 160°F (71°C). Cuts into 6 wedges.

1 wedge: 370 Calories; 19.0 g Total Fat (8.0 g Mono, 1.0 g Poly, 7.0 g Sat); 115 mg Cholesterol; 15 g Carbohydrate; 2 g Fibre; 26 g Protein; 450 mg Sodium

Pictured at right and on back cover.

1. Corned Beef Casserole, page 32
2. Steak and Onion Pot Pie, page 30
3. Veggie Meatloaf Pie, above

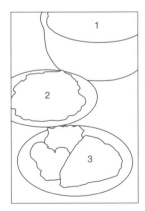

Cabbage Roll Casserole

A delicious lazy cabbage roll casserole with traditional flavours—and a great way to use up leftover beef! Freeze leftovers in portions and reheat in the microwave.

Chopped onion	1 cup	250 mL
Bacon slices, chopped	3	3
Diced cooked roast beef	2 cups	500 mL
Can of diced tomatoes (with juice)	14 oz.	398 mL
Prepared beef broth	1 1/4 cups	300 mL
Can of condensed tomato soup	10 oz.	284 mL
Long-grain white rice	1 cup	250 mL
Dried dillweed	1 tsp.	5 mL
Pepper	1/4 tsp.	1 mL
Shredded cabbage, lightly packed	4 cups	1 L

Cook onion and bacon in large frying pan on medium for about 10 minutes, stirring often, until onion is softened.

Add next 7 ingredients. Heat and stir until boiling. Transfer to greased 9 x 13 inch (23 x 33 cm) baking dish.

Scatter cabbage over beef mixture. Bake, covered, in 350°F (175°C) oven for about 75 minutes, stirring at halftime, until rice is tender. Makes about 10 cups (2.5 L).

1 cup (250 mL): 230 Calories; 9.0 g Total Fat (5.0 g Mono, 1.0 g Poly, 4.5 g Sat); 35 mg Cholesterol; 25 g Carbohydrate; 1 g Fibre; 14 g Protein; 500 mg Sodium

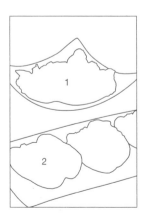

1. Ginger Beef and Broccoli, page 39
2. Curried Beef-Stuffed Peppers, page 40

Potato-Topped Meatloaf

A casserole akin to shepherd's pie—this one has a firm meatloaf base so it slices neatly for serving. Leftovers can be frozen in portions and reheated in the microwave.

Cooking oil	1 tsp.	5 mL
Chopped onion	1/2 cup	125 mL
Chopped carrot	1/4 cup	60 mL
Chopped celery	1/4 cup	60 mL
Large egg, fork-beaten	1	1
Fine dry bread crumbs	1/2 cup	125 mL
Salsa	1/2 cup	125 mL
Italian seasoning	1 tsp.	5 mL
Dry mustard	1/2 tsp.	2 mL
Salt	1/2 tsp.	2 mL
Lean ground beef	1 1/2 lbs.	680 g
Chopped peeled potato	4 cups	1 L
Buttermilk	1/3 cup	75 mL
Butter (or hard margarine)	2 tbsp.	30 mL
Salt	1/4 tsp.	1 mL
Pepper	1/4 tsp.	1 mL

Heat cooking oil in medium frying pan on medium. Add next 3 ingredients. Cook for about 5 minutes, stirring often, until vegetables start to soften. Remove from heat. Cool.

Combine next 6 ingredients in large bowl.

Add beef and onion mixture. Mix well. Press into greased 9 x 9 inch (23 x 23 cm) pan. Cook in 350°F (175°C) oven for about 40 minutes until internal temperature reaches 160°F (71°C). Drain. Cover to keep warm.

Pour water into large saucepan until about 1 inch (2.5 cm) deep. Add potato. Cover. Bring to a boil. Reduce heat to medium. Boil gently for 12 to 15 minutes until tender. Drain. Mash.

Add remaining 4 ingredients. Mash. Spread over meatloaf. Broil on top rack in oven for about 4 minutes until golden. Cuts into 6 pieces.

1 piece: 450 Calories; 22.0 g Total Fat (9.0 g Mono, 1.5 g Poly, 9.0 g Sat); 100 mg Cholesterol; 29 g Carbohydrate; 2 g Fibre; 27 g Protein; 580 mg Sodium

Beef

Ginger Beef and Broccoli

Stir-fry flavours with a spicy ginger bite—a tasty and colourful noodle casserole that the whole family will enjoy.

Beef top sirloin steak, trimmed of fat and cut into thin strips	1 lb.	454 g
Prepared beef broth	1 cup	250 mL
Thinly sliced carrot	1 cup	250 mL
Thinly sliced celery	1/2 cup	125 mL
Thick teriyaki basting sauce	3 tbsp.	50 mL
Finely grated ginger root (or 3/4 tsp., 4 mL, ground ginger)	1 tbsp.	15 mL
Sesame oil (for flavour)	1 tsp.	5 mL
Dried crushed chilies	1/4 tsp.	1 mL
Garlic cloves, minced (or 1/2 tsp., 2 mL, powder)	2	2
Water	8 cups	2 L
Salt	1 tsp.	5 mL
Broad egg noodles	3 cups	750 mL
Small broccoli florets	2 cups	500 mL
Sliced red pepper	1 cup	250 mL

Combine first 9 ingredients in greased 9 x 13 inch (23 x 33 cm) baking dish. Bake, covered, in 375°F (190°C) oven for about 30 minutes until carrot and celery start to soften.

Combine water and salt in large saucepan. Bring to a boil. Add noodles. Boil, uncovered, for 4 minutes, stirring occasionally. Drain. Add to beef mixture.

Add broccoli and red pepper. Stir. Bake, covered, for about 10 minutes until broccoli is tender-crisp. Makes about 9 cups (2.25 L).

1 cup (250 mL): 170 Calories; 7.0 g Total Fat (2.5 g Mono, 0 g Poly, 2.5 g Sat); 35 mg Cholesterol; 14 g Carbohydrate; 1 g Fibre; 13 g Protein; 280 mg Sodium

Pictured on page 36.

Curried Beef-Stuffed Peppers

Stuffed peppers are always a show-stopper! These have a beautiful curry flavour that's well balanced with beef, vegetables and sweet coconut rice. Serve with a dollop of plain yogurt.

Can of coconut milk	14 oz.	398 mL
Salt	1/8 tsp.	0.5 mL
Long-grain brown rice	3/4 cup	175 mL
Cooking oil	1 tsp.	5 mL
Lean ground beef	1/2 lb.	225 g
Chopped onion	1 cup	250 mL
Mild curry paste	2 tbsp.	30 mL
Brown sugar, packed	1 tsp.	5 mL
Finely grated ginger root	1 tsp.	5 mL
(or 1/4 tsp., 1 mL, ground ginger)		
Garlic cloves, minced	2	2
(or 1/2 tsp., 2 mL, powder)		
Ground cumin	1/2 tsp.	2 mL
Large egg, fork-beaten	1	1
Chopped fresh spinach leaves,	1 1/2 cups	375 mL
lightly packed		
Frozen peas	1/2 cup	125 mL
Large red peppers, halved lengthwise	3	3

Combine coconut milk and salt in medium saucepan. Bring to a boil. Add rice. Stir. Reduce heat to medium-low. Simmer, covered, for 35 minutes, without stirring. Remove from heat. Let stand, covered, for about 5 minutes until rice is tender.

Heat cooking oil in large frying pan on medium-high. Add beef and onion. Scramble-fry for about 6 minutes until beef is no longer pink. Drain.

Add next 5 ingredients. Heat and stir for about 1 minute until fragrant. Add to rice.

Add next 3 ingredients. Stir.

(continued on next page)

Beef

Arrange pepper halves in greased 9 x 13 inch (23 x 33) baking dish. Fill with beef mixture. Bake, covered, in 375°F (190°C) oven for about 45 minutes until internal temperature of filling reaches 160°F (71°C) and peppers are tender-crisp. Makes 6 stuffed peppers.

1 stuffed pepper: 370 Calories; 21.0 g Total Fat (3.5 g Mono, 1.0 g Poly, 14.0 g Sat); 45 mg Cholesterol; 32 g Carbohydrate; 4 g Fibre; 13 g Protein; 280 mg Sodium

Pictured on page 36.

Beefy Barley Bake

Portobello mushrooms and thyme combine with chewy barley and tender beef to make a warming winter casserole. Serve with broccoli or green beans.

Cooking oil	2 tsp.	10 mL
Boneless beef blade steak, trimmed of fat and cut into 3/4 inch (2 cm) pieces	1 lb.	454 g
Salt	1/4 tsp.	1 mL
Pepper	1/4 tsp.	1 mL
Sliced portobello mushrooms	2 cups	500 mL
Chopped onion	1 1/2 cups	375 mL
Pot barley	1 1/2 cups	375 mL
Chopped carrot	1 cup	250 mL
Sliced celery	1/2 cup	125 mL
Dried thyme	3/4 tsp.	4 mL
Prepared beef broth	3 cups	750 mL
Water	1 cup	250 mL
Worcestershire sauce	1 tbsp.	15 mL

Heat cooking oil in large frying pan on medium-high. Add beef. Sprinkle with salt and pepper. Cook for about 5 minutes, stirring occasionally, until browned. Transfer with slotted spoon to greased 9 x 13 inch (23 x 33 cm) baking dish.

Add next 6 ingredients to same frying pan. Cook for about 5 minutes, stirring often, until onion is softened.

Add remaining 3 ingredients. Heat and stir for 1 minute, scraping any brown bits from bottom of pan. Add to beef. Stir. Bake, covered, in 375°F (190°C) oven for about 90 minutes, stirring at halftime, until beef and barley are tender and liquid is absorbed. Makes about 9 cups (2.25 L).

1 cup (250 mL): 280 Calories; 10.0 g Total Fat (4.0 g Mono, 1.0 g Poly, 3.5 g Sat); 30 mg Cholesterol; 34 g Carbohydrate; 4 g Fibre; 14 g Protein; 430 mg Sodium

Beef

Beef Noodle Casserole

This rich and cheesy casserole makes for a quick, comforting meal for a busy weeknight! Classic, tasty flavours the kids will love.

Water	8 cups	2 L
Salt	1 tsp.	5 mL
Broad egg noodles	3 cups	750 mL
Cooking oil	2 tsp.	10 mL
Lean ground beef	1 lb.	454 g
Chopped onion	1 cup	250 mL
Salt	1/4 tsp.	1 mL
Pepper	1/8 tsp.	0.5 mL
Chopped fresh white mushrooms	1 cup	250 mL
Can of tomato sauce	7 1/2 oz.	213 mL
Chive and onion cream cheese	3/4 cup	175 mL
Dried thyme	1/4 tsp.	1 mL

Combine water and salt in large saucepan. Bring to a boil. Add noodles. Boil, uncovered, for about 5 minutes, stirring occasionally, until tender but firm. Drain, reserving 3/4 cup (175 mL) cooking water. Return noodles to same pot. Cover to keep warm.

Heat cooking oil in large frying pan on medium. Add next 4 ingredients. Scramble-fry for about 10 minutes until beef is no longer pink. Drain.

Add mushrooms. Cook for about 5 minutes, stirring occasionally, until liquid is evaporated. Add to noodles. Stir.

Stir remaining 3 ingredients and reserved cooking water in medium bowl until smooth. Add to noodle mixture. Stir. Transfer to greased 2 quart (2 L) casserole. Bake, covered, in 350°F (175°C) oven for about 40 minutes until heated through. Makes about 6 cups (1.5 L).

1 cup (250 mL): 350 Calories; 17.0 g Total Fat (5.0 g Mono, 1.5 g Poly, 8.0 g Sat); 80 mg Cholesterol; 22 g Carbohydrate; 1 g Fibre; 22 g Protein; 650 mg Sodium

Paré Pointer

We don't need a working majority. We need a majority working.

Taco Salad Casserole

A cheesy taco bake with ground beef and noodles. The fun nacho chip topping will appeal to the entire family, and the convenience of a one-dish meal will appeal to you! Try it with tri-coloured vegetable rotini for a twist.

Water	8 cups	2 L
Salt	1 tsp.	5 mL
Rotini pasta	2 cups	500 mL
Cooking oil	1 tsp.	5 mL
Lean ground beef	1 lb.	454 g
Chopped onion	1/2 cup	125 mL
Taco seasoning mix, stir before measuring	3 tbsp.	50 mL
Water	1/2 cup	125 mL
Chopped tomato	1 cup	250 mL
Finely chopped green pepper	1/4 cup	60 mL
Crushed nacho chips	3/4 cup	175 mL
Grated medium Cheddar cheese	3/4 cup	175 mL

Combine water and salt in large saucepan. Bring to a boil. Add pasta. Boil, uncovered, for 10 minutes, stirring occasionally. Drain. Return to same pot. Cover to keep warm.

Heat cooking oil in large frying pan on medium. Add next 3 ingredients. Scramble-fry for about 5 minutes until beef is no longer pink.

Add water. Cook for 5 minutes, stirring occasionally. Add to pasta.

Add tomato and green pepper. Stir. Transfer to greased 2 quart (2 L) casserole.

Combine chips and cheese in small bowl. Sprinkle over top. Bake, uncovered, in 350°F (175°C) oven for about 30 minutes until heated through and topping is golden. Serves 4.

1 serving: 530 Calories; 25.0 g Total Fat (8.0 g Mono, 1.5 g Poly, 10.0 g Sat); 90 mg Cholesterol; 36 g Carbohydrate; 2 g Fibre; 33 g Protein; 420 mg Sodium

Pictured on page 108.

Bavarian Lasagna

Rich, creamy meat sauce layered with noodles and sauerkraut makes for old-country comfort food! Leftovers can be frozen in portions and reheated in the microwave.

Cooking oil	2 tsp.	10 mL
Lean ground beef	1 lb.	454 g
Uncooked bratwurst sausage, casing removed	1/2 lb.	225 g
Can of condensed cream of celery soup	10 oz.	284 mL
Milk	1 cup	250 mL
Butter (or hard margarine)	2 tbsp.	30 mL
Jar of sauerkraut, drained	28 oz.	796 mL
Chopped onion	1 cup	250 mL
Dry mustard	1 1/2 tsp.	7 mL
Caraway seed, crushed (see Note)	1/2 tsp.	2 mL
All-purpose flour	3 tbsp.	50 mL
Milk	3 cups	750 mL
Oven-ready lasagna noodles	9	9
Grated mozzarella cheese	1 cup	250 mL
Grated Swiss cheese	1 cup	250 mL
Paprika	1/2 tsp.	2 mL

Heat cooking oil in large frying pan on medium-high. Add beef and sausage. Scramble-fry for about 10 minutes until no longer pink. Drain. Add soup and first amount of milk. Stir.

Melt butter in medium saucepan on medium. Add next 4 ingredients. Cook for about 6 minutes, stirring often, until onion is softened.

Add flour. Heat and stir for 1 minute. Slowly add second amount of milk, stirring constantly until smooth. Heat and stir until boiling and thickened.

(continued on next page)

To assemble, layer ingredients in greased 9 x 13 inch (23 x 33 cm) baking dish as follows:

1. 1 cup (250 mL) beef mixture
2. 3 lasagna noodles
3. Half of sauerkraut mixture
4. 1 1/4 cups (300 mL) beef mixture
5. 3 lasagna noodles
6. Remaining beef mixture
7. Remaining lasagna noodles
8. Remaining sauerkraut mixture

Sprinkle remaining 3 ingredients, in order given, over top. Cover with greased foil. Bake in 350°F (175°C) oven for about 50 minutes until noodles are tender. Carefully remove foil. Bake for about 10 minutes until cheese is golden. Let stand, uncovered, for 10 minutes. Cuts into 8 pieces.

1 piece: 560 Calories; 27.0 g Total Fat (8.0 g Mono, 2.5 g Poly, 12.0 g Sat); 105 mg Cholesterol; 39 g Carbohydrate; 1 g Fibre; 38 g Protein; 1360 mg Sodium

Note: To crush caraway seed, place in large resealable freezer bag. Seal bag. Gently hit with flat side of meat mallet or with rolling pin.

Paré Pointer

People are a lot stronger now. Fifty years ago, a strong adult could barely lift a ten-dollar bag of groceries. Now any child can do it!

Oven Beef Stew

An easy beef stew for those nights when you're looking for a trusty one-dish meal. This freezes well, and leftovers can be reheated on the stovetop or in the microwave. Serve with bread or buns.

All-purpose flour	3 tbsp.	50 mL
Stewing beef, trimmed of fat	2 lbs.	900 g
Cooking oil	1 tbsp.	15 mL
Dry (or alcohol-free) red wine	1/2 cup	125 mL
Chopped peeled potato	2 cups	500 mL
Prepared beef broth	2 cups	500 mL
Can of diced tomatoes (with juice)	14 oz.	398 mL
Chopped carrot	1 cup	250 mL
Chopped onion	1 cup	250 mL
Chopped celery	1/2 cup	125 mL
Frozen kernel corn	1/2 cup	125 mL
Italian seasoning	1 tsp.	5 mL
Bay leaf	1	1
Salt	1/2 tsp.	2 mL
Pepper	1/4 tsp.	1 mL

Put flour into large resealable freezer bag. Add half of beef. Seal bag. Toss until coated. Transfer beef to plate. Repeat with remaining beef. Discard any remaining flour.

Heat cooking oil in Dutch oven on medium. Cook beef, in 2 batches, for about 3 minutes, stirring occasionally, until browned. Transfer beef to medium bowl.

Add wine to same pot. Heat and stir, scraping any brown bits from bottom of pan, until boiling.

Add remaining 11 ingredients and beef. Stir. Cook, covered, in 350°F (175°C) oven for about 2 1/2 hours until beef is tender. Remove and discard bay leaf. Makes about 9 cups (2.25 L).

1 cup (250 mL): 250 Calories; 9.0 g Total Fat (3.0 g Mono, 1.5 g Poly, 3.0 g Sat); 49 mg Cholesterol; 15 g Carbohydrate; 2 g Fibre; 25 g Protein; 523 mg Sodium

Cheeseburger Pasta Bake

Kids will go crazy for this casserole! It's loaded with cheesy noodles, beef and bright bites of pickle and tomato. Freeze leftovers in individual portions and reheat in the microwave.

Water	8 cups	2 L
Salt	1 tsp.	5 mL
Rotini pasta	2 1/2 cups	625 mL
Cooking oil	2 tsp.	10 mL
Lean ground beef	1 lb.	454 g
Chopped onion	1 cup	250 mL
Chopped tomato	1 cup	250 mL
Prepared beef broth	3/4 cup	175 mL
Grated medium Cheddar cheese	1/2 cup	125 mL
Mayonnaise	1/4 cup	60 mL
Finely chopped dill pickle	2 tbsp.	30 mL
Ketchup	2 tbsp.	30 mL
Dry mustard	1 tsp.	5 mL
Grated medium Cheddar cheese	1 1/2 cups	375 mL

Combine water and salt in large saucepan. Bring to a boil. Add pasta. Boil, uncovered, for 12 to 14 minutes, stirring occasionally, until tender but firm. Drain. Return to same pot. Cover to keep warm.

Heat cooking oil in large frying pan on medium. Add beef and onion. Scramble-fry for about 10 minutes until beef is no longer pink. Drain. Add to pasta.

Add next 7 ingredients. Stir. Transfer to greased 2 quart (2 L) casserole.

Sprinkle with second amount of cheese. Bake, covered, in 350°F (175°C) oven for about 30 minutes until heated through. Serves 6.

1 serving: 540 Calories; 31.0 g Total Fat (4.5 g Mono, 1.0 g Poly, 12.0 g Sat); 90 mg Cholesterol; 31 g Carbohydrate; 1 g Fibre; 29 g Protein; 570 mg Sodium

Pictured on page 54.

Swiss Steak Braise

A saucy blend of beef, tender veggies and lots of tomato flavour—try it spooned over mashed potatoes. This recipe makes great leftovers—just chill and reheat in the oven or microwave.

Beef inside round steak, trimmed of fat and cut into 8 pieces	2 lbs.	900 g
Salt, sprinkle		
Pepper, sprinkle		
All-purpose flour	1/4 cup	60 mL
Cooking oil	2 tsp.	10 mL
Sliced fresh white mushrooms	2 cups	500 mL
Sliced onion	2 cups	500 mL
Can of diced tomatoes (with juice)	14 oz.	398 mL
Dry (or alcohol-free) red wine	1/2 cup	125 mL
Sun-dried tomatoes in oil, blotted dry, sliced	1/4 cup	60 mL
Worcestershire sauce	1 tsp.	5 mL
Pepper	1/4 tsp.	1 mL
Prepared beef broth	1 cup	250 mL
Sliced green pepper	1 cup	250 mL
Sliced orange pepper	1 cup	250 mL
Sliced yellow pepper	1 cup	250 mL

Sprinkle beef with salt and pepper. Press into flour in small shallow dish until coated. Reserve remaining flour.

Heat cooking oil in Dutch oven on medium-high. Cook beef, in 2 batches, for about 2 minutes per side, until browned. Remove from heat.

Add next 7 ingredients.

Whisk broth and reserved flour in small bowl until smooth. Pour over top. Stir. Cook, covered, in 325°F (160°C) oven for 45 minutes.

Add remaining 3 ingredients. Stir. Cook, covered, for about 45 minutes until beef is tender. Serves 8.

1 serving: 290 Calories; 11.0 g Total Fat (4.5 g Mono, 1.0 g Poly, 4.5 g Sat); 50 mg Cholesterol; 14 g Carbohydrate; 2 g Fibre; 27 g Protein; 390 mg Sodium

Pictured on page 53.

Cheesy Curried Pasta

This all-in-one pasta bake has delicate curry flavour and plenty of cheese.
This recipe uses radiatore, a type of pasta that resembles tiny radiators.

Water	16 cups	4 L
Salt	2 tsp.	10 mL
Radiatore pasta	5 cups	1.25 L
Cooking oil	2 tsp.	10 mL
Boneless, skinless chicken breast halves, cut into 1 inch (2.5 cm) pieces	1 lb.	454 g
Cooking oil	2 tsp.	10 mL
Chopped zucchini (with peel)	2 cups	500 mL
Chopped onion	1 cup	250 mL
Curry powder	2 tsp.	10 mL
Tub of herb and garlic cream cheese	8 oz.	250 g
1% cottage cheese	3/4 cup	175 mL
Grated Asiago cheese	1 cup	250 mL
Grated mozzarella cheese	1 cup	250 mL

Combine water and salt in large pot. Bring to a boil. Add pasta. Boil, uncovered, for 7 to 9 minutes, stirring occasionally, until tender but firm. Drain, reserving 3/4 cup (175 mL) cooking water. Return pasta to same pot. Cover to keep warm.

Heat first amount of cooking oil in large frying pan on medium-high. Add chicken. Cook for about 6 minutes, stirring occasionally, until browned. Add to pasta.

Add second amount of cooking oil to same frying pan. Add zucchini and onion. Cook for about 5 minutes, stirring often, until onion is softened and starting to brown. Add curry powder. Heat and stir for about 1 minute until fragrant. Remove from heat.

Add cream cheese, cottage cheese and reserved cooking water. Stir until cream cheese is melted. Pour over pasta mixture. Stir. Spread evenly in greased 9 x 13 inch (23 x 33 cm) baking dish.

Sprinkle Asiago and mozzarella cheese over top. Bake in 400°F (205°C) oven for about 15 minutes until cheese is melted and golden. Serves 8.

1 serving: 400 Calories; 18.0 g Total Fat (1.0 g Mono, 1.5 g Poly, 9.0 g Sat); 75 mg Cholesterol; 33 g Carbohydrate; 1 g Fibre; 29 g Protein; 550 mg Sodium

Spicy Chicken Enchiladas

Easy to make, and much better than store-bought!

Cooking oil	1 tsp.	5 mL
Chopped onion	1 cup	250 mL
Cans of mild enchilada sauce (10 oz., 284 mL, each)	2	2
Chopped fresh cilantro (or parsley)	2 tbsp.	30 mL
Finely chopped chipotle peppers in adobo sauce (see Tip, below)	1 1/2 tsp.	7 mL
Chopped cooked chicken (see Tip, page 63)	2 cups	500 mL
Chopped yellow pepper	1/2 cup	125 mL
Chopped fresh cilantro (or parsley)	2 tbsp.	30 mL
Corn tortillas (6 inch, 15 cm, diameter)	8	8
Grated Monterey Jack cheese	1 cup	250 mL

Heat cooking oil in medium frying pan on medium. Add onion. Cook for about 5 minutes, stirring often, until softened.

Add next 3 ingredients. Stir. Bring to a boil. Reduce heat to medium-low. Simmer, uncovered, for 5 minutes, stirring occasionally. Remove from heat. Transfer 1/2 cup (125 mL) to small bowl.

Add next 3 ingredients. Stir. Spoon about 1/4 cup (60 mL) along centre of each tortilla. Roll up tightly from bottom to enclose filling, leaving ends open. Spread 2/3 cup (150 mL) remaining sauce mixture in greased shallow 2 quart (2 L) casserole. Arrange enchiladas, seam-side down, over sauce mixture in casserole. Spoon remaining sauce mixture over top.

Sprinkle with cheese. Cover with greased foil. Bake in 350°F (175°C) oven for 40 minutes. Carefully remove foil. Bake for about 10 minutes until cheese is starting to brown. Serves 8.

1 serving: 210 Calories; 8.0 g Total Fat (0 g Mono, 0.5 g Poly, 2.5 g Sat); 40 mg Cholesterol; 19 g Carbohydrate; 4 g Fibre; 16 g Protein; 750 mg Sodium

 tip   Chipotle chili peppers are smoked jalapeño peppers. Be sure to wash your hands after handling. To store any leftover chipotle peppers, divide into recipe-friendly portions and freeze, with sauce, in airtight containers for up to one year.

Peanut Butter Drumsticks

Something deliciously different for the peanut butter lovers in your family!
Drumsticks are coated in a peanutty sauce and baked with rice and veggies.

Cooking oil	1 tsp.	5 mL
Chopped celery	1/2 cup	125 mL
Chopped onion	1/2 cup	125 mL
Converted white rice	1 1/4 cups	300 mL
Chopped red pepper	1 cup	250 mL
Grated carrot	1/2 cup	125 mL
Chopped dark raisins	1/4 cup	60 mL
Chicken drumsticks (3 – 5 oz., 85 – 140 g, each), skin removed	8	8
Prepared chicken broth	1 1/4 cups	300 mL
Coconut milk	1 cup	250 mL
Peanut butter	1/3 cup	75 mL
Mild curry paste	1 tbsp.	15 mL
Lime juice	2 tsp.	10 mL
Chopped salted peanuts	1/4 cup	60 mL
Finely chopped green onion	2 tbsp.	30 mL
Grated lime zest (see Tip, page 150)	1/2 tsp.	2 mL

Heat cooking oil in medium frying pan on medium. Add celery and onion. Cook for about 5 minutes, stirring often, until celery is softened.

Add rice. Heat and stir for 1 minute. Remove from heat.

Add next 3 ingredients. Stir. Transfer to greased 3 quart (3 L) casserole.

Arrange drumsticks over rice mixture.

Whisk next 5 ingredients in small bowl until smooth. Pour over top. Bake, covered, in 375°F (190°C) oven for about 1 hour until rice is tender and internal temperature of chicken reaches 170°F (77°C).

Combine remaining 3 ingredients in small bowl. Sprinkle over top. Serves 4.

1 serving: 720 Calories; 35.0 g Total Fat (4.5 g Mono, 4.0 g Poly, 15.0 g Sat); 80 mg Cholesterol; 71 g Carbohydrate; 4 g Fibre; 36 g Protein; 460 mg Sodium

Country Chicken Stew

A tasty and comforting stew made with a few kitchen staples. Serve it with fresh biscuits to complete the experience.

All-purpose flour	1/3 cup	75 mL
Dried thyme	1/2 tsp.	2 mL
Garlic powder	1/4 tsp.	1 mL
Salt	1/4 tsp.	1 mL
Pepper	1/4 tsp.	1 mL
Boneless, skinless chicken thighs, quartered	1 1/2 lbs.	680 g
Chopped onion	2 cups	500 mL
Chopped peeled potato	2 cups	500 mL
Sliced carrot	2 cups	500 mL
Sliced fresh white mushrooms	2 cups	500 mL
Prepared chicken broth	2 cups	500 mL

Combine first 5 ingredients in large resealable freezer bag. Add chicken. Seal bag. Toss until coated. Transfer chicken to greased 4 quart (4 L) casserole. Reserve remaining flour mixture.

Add next 4 ingredients to chicken.

Whisk broth and reserved flour mixture in small bowl until smooth. Pour over vegetable mixture. Stir. Cook, covered, in 350°F (175°C) oven for about 1 hour until chicken and vegetables are tender. Makes about 12 cups (3 L).

1 cup (250 mL): 120 Calories; 3.0 g Total Fat (0 g Mono, 0 g Poly, 0 g Sat); 40 mg Cholesterol; 11 g Carbohydrate; 1 g Fibre; 13 g Protein; 105 mg Sodium

Pictured at right.

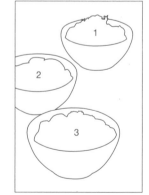

1. Country Chicken Stew, above
2. Swiss Steak Braise, page 48
3. Stout Lamb Stew, page 94

Teriyaki Turkey Casserole

Simple ingredients come together in this noodle casserole with sweet orange
teriyaki sauce and tender-crisp vegetables.

Water	8 cups	2 L
Salt	1 tsp.	5 mL
Medium egg noodles	3 cups	750 mL
Fresh mixed stir-fry vegetables	3 cups	750 mL
Chopped cooked turkey (see Tip, page 65)	1 1/2 cups	375 mL
Orange juice	1 cup	250 mL
Thick teriyaki basting sauce	1/2 cup	125 mL
Sesame oil (for flavour)	1 tsp.	5 mL
Grated orange zest (see Tip, page 150)	1/4 tsp.	1 mL
Pepper	1/4 tsp.	1 mL

Combine water and salt in large saucepan. Bring to a boil. Add noodles. Boil, uncovered, for 5 minutes, stirring occasionally.

Add vegetables. Return to a boil. Cook for 1 minute. Drain.

Add remaining 6 ingredients. Stir. Transfer to greased 2 quart (2 L) casserole. Bake, covered, in 375°F (190°C) oven for about 30 minutes until vegetables are tender-crisp. Makes about 7 cups (1.75 L).

1 cup (250 mL): 170 Calories; 2.0 g Total Fat (0.5 g Mono, 0.5 g Poly, 0.5 g Sat); 45 mg Cholesterol; 24 g Carbohydrate; 1 g Fibre; 13 g Protein; 500 mg Sodium

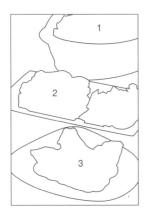

1. Cheeseburger Pasta Bake, page 47
2. Eggplant Parmigiana Lasagna, page 114
3. Seafood Shells in Rosé Sauce, page 82

Cheddar Chicken Crumble

Experience stew in a deliciously unique way. This complete meal-in-one is baked with a cheesy oatmeal crumble topping and gets a little kick from cayenne.

Cooking oil	1 tbsp.	15 mL
Boneless, skinless chicken breast halves, chopped	1 1/2 lbs.	680 g
Cooking oil	1 tsp.	5 mL
Chopped onion	2 cups	500 mL
All-purpose flour	3 tbsp.	50 mL
Prepared chicken broth	3 cups	750 mL
Chopped peeled potato	4 cups	1 L
Sliced carrot	2 cups	500 mL
Bay leaves	3	3
Dried basil	1 1/2 tsp.	7 mL
Cayenne pepper	1/2 tsp.	2 mL
Frozen cut green beans	1 1/2 cups	375 mL
Quick-cooking rolled oats	1 cup	250 mL
Garlic powder	1/2 tsp.	2 mL
Pepper	1/2 tsp.	2 mL
Seasoned salt	1/2 tsp.	2 mL
Cold butter (or hard margarine), cut up	1/4 cup	60 mL
Grated sharp (or medium) Cheddar cheese	1 1/2 cups	375 mL

Heat first amount of cooking oil in large frying pan on medium-high. Add chicken. Cook for about 8 minutes, stirring occasionally, until browned. Transfer to plate. Reduce heat to medium.

Add second amount of cooking oil to same frying pan. Add onion. Cook for about 10 minutes, stirring often, until onion starts to brown.

Add flour. Heat and stir for 1 minute. Slowly add broth, stirring constantly until smooth. Add next 5 ingredients. Stir. Bring to a boil. Reduce heat to medium-low. Simmer, covered, for about 10 minutes, stirring occasionally, until potato is almost tender and sauce is slightly thickened. Remove and discard bay leaves.

(continued on next page)

Add green beans and chicken. Stir. Transfer to greased 9 x 13 inch (23 x 33 cm) baking dish.

Combine next 4 ingredients in medium bowl. Cut in butter until mixture resembles coarse crumbs.

Add cheese. Stir. Sprinkle over chicken mixture. Bake in 375°F (190°C) oven for about 40 minutes until bubbling and topping is golden. Serves 6.

1 serving: 510 Calories; 22.0 g Total Fat (4.5 g Mono, 2.0 g Poly, 11.0 g Sat); 130 mg Cholesterol; 40 g Carbohydrate; 6 g Fibre; 40 g Protein; 620 mg Sodium

Fiesta Turkey Strata

Find a home for holiday leftovers in this flavourful strata! If you're busy with houseguests, this can be prepared a day in advance. Use a round casserole dish to best fit the tortillas.

Finely chopped cooked turkey (see Tip, page 65)	2 cups	500 mL
Chopped red pepper	1/2 cup	125 mL
Can of diced green chilies	4 oz.	113 g
Sliced green onion	1/4 cup	60 mL
Flour tortillas (9 inch, 23 cm, diameter)	6	6
Large eggs	4	4
Milk	2 cups	500 mL
Chili powder	1 tsp.	5 mL
Ground cumin	1/2 tsp.	2 mL
Grated jalapeño Monterey Jack cheese	1 1/2 cups	375 mL

Combine first 4 ingredients in medium bowl.

Place 1 tortilla in greased 3 quart (3 L) casserole. Fold edges to fit if necessary. Scatter about 2/3 cup (150 mL) turkey mixture over tortilla. Repeat with remaining tortillas and turkey mixture, ending with tortilla.

Whisk next 4 ingredients in same medium bowl. Pour over top.

Sprinkle with cheese. Chill, covered, for at least 6 hours or overnight. Bake, uncovered, in 350°F (175°C) oven for about 75 minutes until puffed and golden. Let stand for 10 minutes. Cuts into 8 wedges.

1 wedge: 380 Calories; 14.0 g Total Fat (3.5 g Mono, 1.0 g Poly, 6.0 g Sat); 120 mg Cholesterol; 36 g Carbohydrate; 2 g Fibre; 25 g Protein; 550 mg Sodium

Three-Cheese Lasagna

Any true fromage *enthusiast will be awestruck by this creamy ricotta, mozzarella and Asiago creation—and it's a one-dish meal to boot!*

Cooking oil	1 tbsp.	15 mL
Lean ground chicken	1 lb.	454 g
Chopped onion	1 cup	250 mL
Chopped red pepper	2 cups	500 mL
Sliced fresh white mushrooms	2 cups	500 mL
Garlic cloves, minced	2	2
(or 1/2 tsp., 2 mL, powder)		
Salt	1/2 tsp.	2 mL
Pepper	1/4 tsp.	1 mL
Can of diced tomatoes (with juice)	14 oz.	398 mL
Large eggs, fork-beaten	2	2
Ricotta cheese	4 cups	1 L
Grated Asiago cheese	1/2 cup	125 mL
Basil pesto	1/3 cup	75 mL
Ground nutmeg	1/4 tsp.	1 mL
Pepper, sprinkle		
Oven-ready lasagna noodles	12	12
Grated Asiago cheese	1 cup	250 mL
Grated mozzarella cheese	1 cup	250 mL

Heat cooking oil in large frying pan on medium-high. Add chicken and onion. Scramble-fry for about 5 minutes until chicken is no longer pink.

Add next 5 ingredients. Cook for about 8 minutes, stirring occasionally, until vegetables are softened and liquid is evaporated.

Add tomatoes. Stir. Remove from heat.

Combine next 6 ingredients in large bowl.

(continued on next page)

To assemble, layer ingredients in greased 9 x 13 inch (23 x 33 cm) baking dish as follows:

1. 4 lasagna noodles
2. Half of chicken mixture
3. Half of ricotta cheese mixture
4. 4 lasagna noodles
5. Remaining chicken mixture
6. Remaining lasagna noodles
7. Remaining ricotta cheese mixture

Sprinkle second amount of Asiago and mozzarella cheese over top. Cover with greased foil. Bake in 350°F (175°C) oven for 45 minutes. Carefully remove foil. Bake for about 20 minutes until noodles are tender and cheese is golden. Let stand for 15 minutes. Cuts into 8 pieces.

1 piece: 660 Calories; 33.0 g Total Fat (4.0 g Mono, 1.5 g Poly, 12.0 g Sat); 140 mg Cholesterol; 48 g Carbohydrate; 2 g Fibre; 42 g Protein; 870 mg Sodium

---

Mom's Chicken Casserole

Throw this easy chicken casserole together for a convenient weeknight meal. There'll be plenty of sauce for serving over pasta, rice or potatoes.

Boneless, skinless chicken thighs, halved	1 lb.	454 g
Can of diced tomatoes (with juice)	14 oz.	398 mL
Alfredo pasta sauce	1 cup	250 mL
Chopped fresh white mushrooms	1 cup	250 mL
Chopped onion	1/2 cup	125 mL
Pepper, sprinkle		
Sliced green onion	2 tbsp.	30 mL
Chopped fresh parsley	1 tbsp.	15 mL
(or 3/4 tsp., 4 mL, flakes)		

Arrange chicken in greased 2 quart (2 L) casserole.

Combine next 5 ingredients in medium bowl. Pour over chicken. Cook, covered, in 350°F (175°C) oven for about 1 hour until chicken is no longer pink inside.

Sprinkle with green onion and parsley. Makes about 4 cups (1 L).

1 cup (250 mL): 260 Calories; 13.0 g Total Fat (0 g Mono, 0 g Poly, 4.5 g Sat); 105 mg Cholesterol; 11 g Carbohydrate; trace Fibre; 27 g Protein; 570 mg Sodium

Buffalo Chicken Casserole

A unique incarnation of a familiar flavour combination—a spicy chicken stew with a delicious blue cheese biscuit topping. Serve with beer and your sport of choice!

Cooking oil	1 tsp.	5 mL
Boneless, skinless chicken thighs, halved	2 lbs.	900 g
Cooking oil	1 tsp.	5 mL
Chopped onion	1 cup	250 mL
Garlic cloves, minced	2	2
(or 1/2 tsp., 2 mL, powder)		
Salt	1/4 tsp.	1 mL
Pepper	1/8 tsp.	0.5 mL
All-purpose flour	3 tbsp.	50 mL
Prepared chicken broth	1 cup	250 mL
Louisiana hot sauce	1/4 cup	60 mL
Sliced baby potato	2 cups	500 mL
Sliced carrot	2 cups	500 mL
Sliced celery	1 cup	250 mL
BLUE CHEESE BISCUITS		
Biscuit mix	2 cups	500 mL
Crumbled blue cheese	1/4 cup	60 mL
Chopped fresh parsley	2 tbsp.	30 mL
(or 1 tsp., 5 mL, flakes)		
Milk	1 cup	250 mL

Heat first amount of cooking oil in large frying pan on medium-high. Cook chicken, in 2 batches, for about 10 minutes, stirring occasionally, until browned. Transfer chicken to greased 3 quart (3 L) casserole. Reduce heat to medium.

Heat second amount of cooking oil in same frying pan. Add next 4 ingredients. Cook for about 5 minutes, stirring often, until onion starts to brown.

Add flour. Heat and stir for 1 minute. Slowly add broth, stirring constantly until smooth. Heat and stir until boiling and thickened. Add hot sauce. Stir. Add to chicken.

(continued on next page)

Chicken & Turkey

Add next 3 ingredients. Stir. Bake, covered, in 375°F (190°C) oven for about 1 hour until potato and carrot are tender. Stir.

Blue Cheese Biscuits: Combine first 3 ingredients in medium bowl. Make a well in centre.

Add milk. Stir until just moistened. Drop batter onto hot chicken mixture in 8 mounds, using about 1/4 cup (60 mL) for each. Bake, uncovered, for about 20 minutes until wooden pick inserted in centre of biscuit comes out clean. Serves 8.

1 serving: 373 Calories; 8.0 g Total Fat (0.5 g Mono, 1.0 g Poly, 1.0 g Sat); 86 mg Cholesterol; 43 g Carbohydrate; 3 g Fibre; 29 g Protein; 570 mg Sodium

Sweet-and-Sour Chicken Bake

An easy recipe that uses basic ingredients to create a sweet-and-sour casserole that the kids will love. Spoon over chow mein noodles or steamed rice.

Cooking oil	1 tsp.	5 mL
Boneless, skinless chicken thighs, quartered	1 lb.	454 g
Bag of frozen California mixed vegetables, thawed	1 lb.	454 g
Can of cut baby corn, drained	14 oz.	398 mL
Plum sauce	1 cup	250 mL
Apple cider vinegar	3 tbsp.	50 mL
Finely grated ginger root (or 1/4 tsp., 1 mL, ground ginger)	1 tsp.	5 mL
Garlic clove, minced (or 1/4 tsp., 1 mL, powder)	1	1
Roasted sesame seeds	2 tsp.	10 mL

Heat cooking oil in large frying pan on medium-high. Add chicken. Cook for about 5 minutes, stirring often, until browned. Transfer to ungreased 3 quart (3 L) casserole.

Add next 6 ingredients. Stir. Cook, covered, in 375°F (190°C) oven for about 40 minutes until vegetables are tender-crisp and chicken is no longer pink inside. Stir.

Sprinkle with sesame seeds. Makes about 7 cups (1.75 L).

1 cup (250 mL): 250 Calories; 5.0 g Total Fat (0.5 g Mono, 1.0 g Poly, 0 g Sat); 45 mg Cholesterol; 37 g Carbohydrate; 4 g Fibre; 15 g Protein; 270 mg Sodium

Chicken Leek Pie

Put leftover chicken and potato to good use in this one-dish meal that's topped with a beautiful golden crust—very inviting.

Butter (or hard margarine)	2 tbsp.	30 mL
Thinly sliced leek (white part only)	2 cups	500 mL
Garlic clove, minced	1	1
(or 1/4 tsp., 1 mL, powder)		
Salt	1/8 tsp.	0.5 mL
Pepper	1/4 tsp.	1 mL
Poultry seasoning	1/4 tsp.	1 mL
All-purpose flour	1 tbsp.	15 mL
Prepared chicken broth	1 cup	250 mL
Milk	1/4 cup	60 mL
Chopped cooked chicken (see Tip, page 63)	3 cups	750 mL
Diced peeled cooked potato	1 cup	250 mL
Frozen mixed vegetables, thawed	1 cup	250 mL
Pastry for 9 inch (23 cm) pie shell		
Large egg, fork-beaten	1	1

Melt butter in large frying pan on medium. Add next 5 ingredients. Cook for about 8 minutes, stirring often, until leek is softened.

Add flour. Heat and stir for 1 minute. Slowly add broth, stirring constantly until smooth. Add milk. Heat and stir until boiling and thickened. Remove from heat.

Add next 3 ingredients. Stir. Spread evenly in greased 9 inch (23 cm) pie plate. Cool.

Roll out pastry on lightly floured surface to about 1/8 inch (3 mm) thickness. Place over chicken mixture. Trim and crimp decorative edge to seal. Brush top with egg. Cut several small vents in top to allow steam to escape. Bake in 375°F (190°C) oven for about 45 minutes until pastry is golden. Let stand on wire rack for 10 minutes. Cuts into 6 wedges.

1 wedge: 340 Calories; 17.0 g Total Fat (4.5 g Mono, 1.0 g Poly, 4.5 g Sat); 90 mg Cholesterol; 24 g Carbohydrate; 2 g Fibre; 22 g Protein; 280 mg Sodium

Turkey Rice Casserole

All your favourite festive flavours in one convenient casserole. Tender turkey,
sweet cranberries and nutty brown rice make a filling autumn meal.

Bacon slices, chopped	4	4
Prepared chicken broth	1 1/2 cups	375 mL
Chopped onion	1 cup	250 mL
Long-grain brown rice	1 cup	250 mL
Chopped celery	1/2 cup	125 mL
Dry (or alcohol-free) white wine	1/4 cup	60 mL
Dried sage	1/2 tsp.	2 mL
Dried thyme	1/2 tsp.	2 mL
Boneless, skinless turkey thighs, cut into 1 inch (2.5 cm) pieces	1 1/2 lbs.	680 g
Salt	1/4 tsp.	1 mL
Pepper	1/4 tsp.	1 mL
Chopped dried cranberries	1/4 cup	60 mL
Chopped fresh parsley	2 tbsp.	30 mL

Cook bacon in large frying pan on medium, stirring often, until crisp.
Transfer with slotted spoon to paper towel-lined plate to drain. Transfer to
greased 3 quart (3 L) casserole. Discard drippings from pan.

Add next 7 ingredients. Stir.

Sprinkle turkey with salt and pepper. Arrange over rice mixture. Bake,
covered, in 375°F (190°C) oven for about 90 minutes, stirring at halftime,
until rice is tender.

Sprinkle with cranberries and parsley. Stir. Makes about 6 cups (1.5 L).

1 cup (250 mL): 317 Calories; 9.0 g Total Fat (3.5 g Mono, 1.5 g Poly 2.5 g Sat); 101 mg Cholesterol;
28 g Carbohydrate; 2 g Fibre; 26 g Protein; 375 mg Sodium

 tip Don't have any leftover chicken? Start with 2 boneless, skinless
chicken breast halves (4 – 6 oz., 113 – 170 g, each). Place in large
frying pan with 1 cup (250 mL) water or chicken broth. Simmer,
covered, for 12 to 14 minutes until no longer pink inside. Drain.
Chop. Makes about 2 cups (500 mL) cooked chicken.

Turkey Pastitsio

We've put the lamb out to pasture! Our turkey version of pastitsio (pronounced pah-STEET-see-oh) is a lighter take on the Greek favourite. A complete meal with added vegetables and whole-wheat pasta.

Water	12 cups	3 L
Salt	1 1/2 tsp.	7 mL
Whole-wheat elbow macaroni	3 cups	750 mL
Olive (or cooking) oil	2 tbsp.	30 mL
Lean ground turkey	1 lb.	454 g
Diced zucchini (with peel)	1 1/2 cups	375 mL
Grated carrot	1 cup	250 mL
Chopped onion	2/3 cup	150 mL
Dried oregano	1 tsp.	5 mL
Ground cinnamon	1 tsp.	5 mL
Garlic cloves, minced	2	2
(or 1/2 tsp., 2 mL, powder)		
Dried thyme	1/2 tsp.	2 mL
Salt	1/2 tsp.	2 mL
Pepper	1/4 tsp.	1 mL
Can of diced tomatoes (with juice)	14 oz.	398 mL
Tomato paste (see Tip, page 111)	3 tbsp.	50 mL
Grated Parmesan cheese	1/4 cup	60 mL
Butter (or hard margarine)	3 tbsp.	50 mL
All-purpose flour	1/4 cup	60 mL
Milk	3 cups	750 mL
Large egg, fork-beaten	1	1
Ricotta cheese	1 cup	250 mL
Salt	1/2 tsp.	2 mL
Pepper	1/2 tsp.	2 mL
Ground nutmeg	1/8 tsp.	0.5 mL

(continued on next page)

Combine water and salt in Dutch oven. Bring to a boil. Add pasta. Boil, uncovered, for 8 to 10 minutes, stirring occasionally, until tender but firm. Drain, reserving 1/2 cup (125 mL) cooking water. Return pasta to same pot. Cover to keep warm.

Heat olive oil in large frying pan on medium. Add next 10 ingredients. Scramble-fry for about 12 minutes until turkey is no longer pink.

Add tomatoes, tomato paste and reserved cooking water. Stir. Bring to a boil. Reduce heat to medium-low. Simmer, covered, for 5 minutes to blend flavours. Add to pasta. Stir. Spread evenly in greased 9 x 13 inch (23 x 33 cm) baking dish.

Sprinkle with Parmesan cheese.

Melt butter in medium saucepan on medium. Add flour. Heat and stir for 1 minute. Slowly add milk, stirring constantly until smooth. Heat and stir until boiling and thickened. Remove from heat.

Add remaining 5 ingredients. Stir until well combined. Pour over top. Bake in 350°F (175°C) oven for about 50 minutes until edges are golden. Serves 8.

1 serving: 460 Calories; 19.0 g Total Fat (5.0 g Mono, 1.0 g Poly, 8.0 g Sat); 90 mg Cholesterol; 49 g Carbohydrate; 5 g Fibre; 28 g Protein; 730 mg Sodium

 tip Don't have any leftover turkey? Start with 1 boneless, skinless turkey breast (about 10 oz., 285 g). Place in large frying pan with 1 cup (250 mL) water or chicken broth. Simmer, covered, for 12 to 14 minutes until no longer pink inside. Drain. Chop. Makes about 2 cups (500 mL) cooked turkey.

Chicken Provençal

Tender chicken with a complex tomato sauce and plenty of peppers and olives. This saucy main course can be served with potatoes or over your favourite pasta or rice.

All-purpose flour	1/3 cup	75 mL
Salt	1/4 tsp.	1 mL
Pepper	1/2 tsp.	2 mL
Bone-in chicken thighs (5 – 6 oz., 140 – 170 g, each), skin removed	8	8
Olive (or cooking) oil	1 tbsp.	15 mL
Sliced fresh white mushrooms	1 1/2 cups	375 mL
Chopped green pepper	1/2 cup	125 mL
Chopped onion	1/2 cup	125 mL
Garlic cloves, minced (or 1/2 tsp., 2 mL, powder)	2	2
Dry (or alcohol-free) white wine	1/2 cup	125 mL
Can of diced tomatoes (with juice)	14 oz.	398 mL
Dried marjoram	1 tsp.	5 mL
Granulated sugar	1/4 tsp.	1 mL
Chopped kalamata olives (optional)	2 tbsp.	30 mL

Combine first 3 ingredients in large resealable freezer bag. Add chicken. Seal bag. Toss until coated. Transfer chicken to plate. Reserve remaining flour mixture.

Heat olive oil in large frying pan on medium-high. Add chicken. Cook for about 5 minutes, turning occasionally, until browned. Transfer with slotted spoon to ungreased 3 quart (3 L) casserole. Reduce heat to medium.

Add next 4 ingredients to same frying pan. Cook for about 5 minutes, stirring often, until liquid is evaporated. Sprinkle with reserved flour mixture. Heat and stir for 1 minute.

Add wine. Heat and stir, scraping any brown bits from bottom of pan, until boiling. Add next 3 ingredients. Stir. Pour over chicken. Cook, covered, in 350°F (175°C) oven for about 35 minutes until internal temperature of chicken reaches 170°F (77°C).

Sprinkle with olives. Serves 4.

(continued on next page)

1 serving: 390 Calories; 14.0 g Total Fat (3.0 g Mono, 0 g Poly, 0.5 g Sat); 150 mg Cholesterol; 16 g Carbohydrate; 2 g Fibre; 43 g Protein; 440 mg Sodium

Pictured on page 71.

Curry Chicken Stew

A very approachable, not-too-spicy curry with tender chicken, vegetables and a sweet broth to serve over rice. If you'd like it spicier, use a hot curry paste. Reheat leftovers on the stovetop or in the microwave.

Boneless, skinless chicken thighs, quartered	2 lbs.	900 g
Chopped peeled orange-fleshed sweet potato	2 cups	500 mL
Can of diced tomatoes (with juice)	14 oz.	398 mL
Chopped dried apricot	1/2 cup	125 mL
Cooking oil	2 tsp.	10 mL
Chopped onion	2 cups	500 mL
Sliced fresh white mushrooms	2 cups	500 mL
Chopped carrot	1 cup	250 mL
Mild curry paste	2 tbsp.	30 mL
Garlic cloves, minced (or 1/2 tsp., 2 mL, powder)	2	2
Salt	1/2 tsp.	2 mL
Pepper	1/2 tsp.	2 mL
All-purpose flour	1 tbsp.	15 mL
Prepared chicken broth	1 cup	250 mL

Stir first 4 ingredients in greased 9 x 13 inch (23 x 33 cm) baking dish.

Heat cooking oil in large frying pan on medium. Add next 3 ingredients. Cook for about 10 minutes, stirring often, until onion is softened.

Add next 4 ingredients. Heat and stir for about 1 minute until fragrant.

Add flour. Heat and stir for 1 minute. Slowly add broth, stirring constantly until smooth. Heat and stir until boiling and thickened. Add to chicken mixture. Stir. Cook, covered, in 350°F (175°C) oven for about 90 minutes until vegetables are tender. Makes about 12 cups (3 L).

1 cup (250 mL): 160 Calories; 4.5 g Total Fat (0 g Mono, 0 g Poly, 0 g Sat); 55 mg Cholesterol; 14 g Carbohydrate; 2 g Fibre; 16 g Protein; 320 mg Sodium

Tasty Turkey Tetrazzini

An excellent way to use up all those turkey leftovers—no one will turn down creamy spaghetti! You could also use broth in place of wine if you prefer.

Water	12 cups	3 L
Salt	1 1/2 tsp.	7 mL
Spaghetti	8 oz.	225 g
Cooking oil	1 tsp.	5 mL
Sliced fresh white mushrooms	1 cup	250 mL
Chopped onion	1/2 cup	125 mL
Prepared chicken broth	1 cup	250 mL
Block cream cheese, softened	4 oz.	125 g
Dry (or alcohol-free) white wine	1/4 cup	60 mL
Salt	1/4 tsp.	1 mL
Pepper	1/4 tsp.	1 mL
Diced cooked turkey (see Tip, page 65)	2 cups	500 mL
Frozen peas	1 cup	250 mL
Diced red pepper	1/2 cup	125 mL
Sour cream	1/2 cup	125 mL
Grated Parmesan cheese	1/4 cup	60 mL

Combine water and salt in Dutch oven. Bring to a boil. Add pasta. Boil, uncovered, for 10 to 12 minutes, stirring occasionally, until tender but firm. Drain. Return to same pot. Cover to keep warm.

Heat cooking oil in large frying pan on medium. Add mushrooms and onion. Cook for about 8 minutes, stirring often, until onion is softened and liquid is evaporated.

Add next 5 ingredients. Heat and stir until smooth.

Add next 4 ingredients. Stir. Add to pasta. Toss. Transfer to greased 3 quart (3 L) casserole.

Sprinkle Parmesan cheese over top. Bake, covered, in 375°F (190°C) oven for 30 minutes. Remove cover. Bake for about 10 minutes until bubbling and golden. Stir. Makes about 8 cups (2 L).

1 cup (250 mL): 280 Calories; 11.0 g Total Fat (1.0 g Mono, 1.0 g Poly, 5.0 g Sat); 50 mg Cholesterol; 27 g Carbohydrate; 2 g Fibre; 18 g Protein; 250 mg Sodium

Pictured on page 71.

Potato Tot Shepherd's Pie

Cute potato tots top a mix of turkey and veggies in this fun, kid-friendly casserole.

Cooking oil	2 tsp.	10 mL
Lean ground turkey	1 1/2 lbs.	680 g
Dried thyme	1 tsp.	5 mL
Dried oregano	1/2 tsp.	2 mL
Garlic powder	1/4 tsp.	1 mL
Salt	1/4 tsp.	1 mL
Pepper	1/4 tsp.	1 mL
Cooking oil	1 tsp.	5 mL
Chopped onion	1 1/2 cups	375 mL
Chopped carrot	1 cup	250 mL
Chopped celery	1/2 cup	125 mL
All-purpose flour	2 tbsp.	30 mL
Milk	1 cup	250 mL
Prepared chicken broth	3/4 cup	175 mL
Dijon mustard	1 tbsp.	15 mL
Frozen peas	1 cup	250 mL
Frozen potato tots (gems or puffs)	6 cups	1.5 L

Heat first amount of cooking oil in large frying pan on medium-high. Add next 6 ingredients. Scramble-fry for about 8 minutes until turkey is no longer pink. Spread evenly in greased 9 x 13 inch (23 x 33 cm) pan. Reduce heat to medium.

Heat second amount of cooking oil in same frying pan. Add next 3 ingredients. Cook for about 10 minutes, stirring often, until onion is softened.

Add flour. Heat and stir for 1 minute. Slowly add milk, stirring constantly until smooth. Add broth and mustard. Heat and stir until boiling and thickened.

Add peas. Stir. Spoon over turkey mixture.

Arrange potato tots over top. Bake in 350°F (175°C) oven for about 1 hour until potato tots are golden. Serves 6.

1 serving: 510 Calories; 26.0 g Total Fat (5.0 g Mono, 2.0 g Poly, 9.0 g Sat); 90 mg Cholesterol; 45 g Carbohydrate; 6 g Fibre; 28 g Protein; 1150 mg Sodium

Pictured on page 108.

Spinach Basil Chicken

Simple ingredients like fresh basil and tasty tomatoes create a satisfying combination. You can use broth in place of wine if you prefer.

Boneless, skinless chicken breast halves, cut into 1 1/2 inch (3.8 cm) pieces	1 lb.	454 g
Chopped fresh spinach leaves, lightly packed	1 1/2 cups	375 mL
Prepared chicken broth	1 1/2 cups	375 mL
Chopped seeded tomato	1 cup	250 mL
White basmati rice	1 cup	250 mL
Dry (or alcohol-free) white wine	1/4 cup	60 mL
Chopped fresh basil (or 1 tsp., 5 mL, dried)	2 tbsp.	30 mL
Cooking oil	2 tsp.	10 mL
Garlic clove, minced (or 1/4 tsp., 1 mL, powder)	1	1
Salt	1/4 tsp.	1 mL
Pepper	1/4 tsp.	1 mL

Toss all 11 ingredients in large bowl. Transfer to greased 2 quart (2 L) casserole. Bake, covered, in 375°F (190°C) oven for about 45 minutes, stirring at halftime, until rice is tender and chicken is no longer pink inside. Let stand, covered, for about 10 minutes until liquid is absorbed. Makes about 6 cups (1.5 L).

1 cup (250 mL): 220 Calories; 3.0 g Total Fat (1.0 g Mono, 1.0 g Poly, 0.5 g Sat); 55 mg Cholesterol; 27 g Carbohydrate; trace Fibre; 22 g Protein; 200 mg Sodium

Pictured at right.

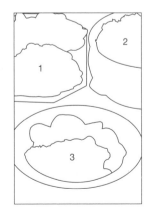

1. Tasty Turkey Tetrazzini, page 68
2. Spinach Basil Chicken, above
3. Chicken Provençal, page 66

Chicken & Turkey

Beautiful Poached Halibut

An attractive arrangement of halibut stacked with colourful peppers and ham. Spoon the cooking liquid over individual servings for added flavour.

Cooking oil	1 tsp.	5 mL
Thinly sliced red pepper	1 cup	250 mL
Thinly sliced yellow pepper	1 cup	250 mL
Deli ham, cut into thin strips	4 oz.	113 g
Garlic clove, minced (or 1/4 tsp., 1 mL, powder)	1	1
Halibut fillets, any small bones removed (about 1 lb., 454 g)	4	4
Dry (or alcohol-free) white wine	1/2 cup	125 mL
Lemon juice	2 tbsp.	30 mL
Salt	1/8 tsp.	0.5 mL
Pepper	1/8 tsp.	0.5 mL

Heat cooking oil in large frying pan on medium. Add next 4 ingredients. Cook for about 5 minutes, stirring often, until peppers are tender-crisp.

Arrange fillets in greased 9 x 13 inch (23 x 33 cm) baking dish.

Combine remaining 4 ingredients in small cup. Pour over fillets. Scatter pepper mixture over top. Cook, covered, in 375°F (190°C) oven for about 25 minutes until fish flakes easily when tested with fork. Serves 4.

1 serving: 200 Calories; 5.0 g Total Fat (1.5 g Mono, 1.0 g Poly, 0.5 g Sat); 49 mg Cholesterol; 4 g Carbohydrate; 1 g Fibre; 29 g Protein; 353 mg Sodium

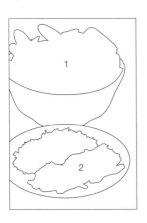

Pictured at left.

1. Thai Curry Mussels, page 75
2. Beautiful Poached Halibut, above

Tandoori Salmon Bake

The delicious flavours of curry paste, applesauce and yogurt come together to create a salmon bake with a rustic appearance.

Large egg, fork-beaten	1	1
Cooked white basmati rice	3 cups	750 mL
(about 1 cup, 250 mL, uncooked)		
Salt	1/4 tsp.	1 mL
Pepper	1/4 tsp.	1 mL
Cooking oil	1 tsp.	5 mL
Chopped celery	1 cup	250 mL
Chopped onion	1 cup	250 mL
Garlic cloves, minced	2	2
(or 1/2 tsp., 2 mL, powder)		
Tandoori curry paste	2 tbsp.	30 mL
Salt	1/2 tsp.	2 mL
Salmon fillets, skin and any small bones	1 lb.	454 g
removed, cut into 1 inch (2.5 cm) pieces		
Sweetened applesauce	1/4 cup	60 mL
Plain yogurt	3 tbsp.	50 mL

Combine first 4 ingredients in medium bowl. Press into greased 2 quart (2 L) casserole.

Heat cooking oil in large frying pan on medium. Add next 3 ingredients. Cook for about 10 minutes, stirring often, until celery is tender.

Add curry paste and salt. Heat and stir for 1 minute. Remove from heat.

Add remaining 3 ingredients. Stir. Spread over rice mixture. Bake, uncovered, in 350°F (175°C) oven for about 30 minutes until fish flakes easily when tested with fork. Serves 4.

1 serving: 420 Calories; 11.0 g Total Fat (3.5 g Mono, 3.5 g Poly, 1.5 g Sat); 100 mg Cholesterol; 52 g Carbohydrate; 1 g Fibre; 29 g Protein; 740 mg Sodium

Paré Pointer

My dog is pretty dirty, but he's even prettier when he's clean.

Fish & Seafood

Thai Curry Mussels

Mussel lovers unite! These mussels have a tasty coconut curry sauce, topped with a sprinkle of fresh tomato and herbs. Serve with plenty of crusty white bread.

Fresh mussels, scrubbed clean (see Note 1)	2 lbs.	900 g
Can of coconut milk	14 oz.	398 mL
Lime juice	2 tbsp.	30 mL
Thai red curry paste	2 tsp.	10 mL
Finely grated ginger root	1 tsp.	5 mL
(or 1/4 tsp., 1 mL, ground ginger)		
Dried crushed chilies	1/4 tsp.	1 mL
Salt	1/8 tsp.	0.5 mL
Chopped seeded tomato	1/4 cup	60 mL
Chopped fresh basil	1 tbsp.	15 mL
Chopped fresh cilantro (or parsley)	1 tbsp.	15 mL

Lightly tap any mussels that are opened 1/4 inch (6 mm) or more. Discard any that do not close (see Note 2). Place mussels in 9 x 13 inch (23 x 33 cm) pan.

Whisk next 6 ingredients in small saucepan. Bring to a boil, stirring occasionally. Pour over mussels. Cover tightly with foil. Cook in 400°F (205°C) oven for about 12 minutes until mussels are opened. Carefully remove foil. Discard any unopened mussels.

Sprinkle with remaining 3 ingredients. Serves 4.

1 serving: 382 Calories; 26.0 g Total Fat (2.0 g Mono, 1.5 g Poly, 20.0 g Sat); 65 mg Cholesterol; 14 g Carbohydrate; 1 g Fibre; 27 g Protein; 830 mg Sodium

Pictured on page 72.

Note 1: Remove the "beard," the stringy fibres attached to the shell, either by clipping them or giving them a sharp tug out the hinge end of the mussel (not the open end).

Note 2: For safety reasons, it is important to discard any mussels that do not close before cooking, as well as any that have not opened during cooking.

Sole and Oyster Casserole

This recipe is truly for the seafood lovers! Smoked oysters are included as a flavourful companion for sole in this hearty one-dish meal.

Cooking oil	1 tsp.	5 mL
Chopped fresh white mushrooms	1 cup	250 mL
Finely chopped celery	1/2 cup	125 mL
Finely chopped onion	1/2 cup	125 mL
Cooked long-grain white rice (about 3/4 cup, 175 mL, uncooked)	2 1/2 cups	625 mL
Can of condensed cream of mushroom soup	10 oz.	284 mL
Sour cream	1 cup	250 mL
Chopped fresh chives (or green onion)	1/4 cup	60 mL
Lemon juice	2 tbsp.	30 mL
Can of smoked oysters, drained and chopped	3 oz.	85 g
Sole fillets, any small bones removed	1 lb.	454 g
Chopped fresh chives (or green onion)	2 tbsp.	30 mL

Heat cooking oil in large frying pan on medium. Add next 3 ingredients. Cook for about 8 minutes, stirring often, until onion is browned and liquid is evaporated.

Add rice. Heat and stir for about 2 minutes until heated through.

Stir next 4 ingredients in medium bowl until smooth. Reserve 1 cup (250 mL) in small bowl. Add remaining soup mixture to rice mixture.

Add oysters. Stir.

To assemble, layer ingredients in ungreased 8 x 8 inch (20 x 20 cm) baking dish as follows:

1. Half of rice mixture
2. Half of fillets
3. Remaining rice mixture
4. Remaining fillets
5. Reserved soup mixture

Bake, covered, in 375°F (190°C) oven for 30 minutes. Bake, uncovered, for about 25 minutes until fish flakes easily when tested with fork.

(continued on next page)

Fish & Seafood

Sprinkle with second amount of chives. Serves 6.

1 serving: 310 Calories; 12.0 g Total Fat (0.5 g Mono, 0 g Poly, 4.5 g Sat); 60 mg Cholesterol; 29 g Carbohydrate; 1 g Fibre; 21 g Protein; 500 mg Sodium

Risotto Marinara

There's no constant stirring involved in constructing this risotto—this is a bold and spicy oven-baked version with lots of creamy rice, seafood and lemony flavour. You may use broth in place of wine if you prefer.

Arborio rice	1 cup	250 mL
Finely chopped onion	1/2 cup	125 mL
Grated zucchini (with peel)	1/2 cup	125 mL
Cooking oil	2 tsp.	10 mL
Garlic cloves, minced	2	2
(or 1/2 tsp., 2 mL, powder)		
Salt	1/8 tsp.	0.5 mL
Pepper	1/4 tsp.	1 mL
Dried crushed chilies	1/8 tsp.	0.5 mL
Prepared vegetable broth	2 1/4 cups	550 mL
Dry (or alcohol-free) white wine	1/2 cup	125 mL
Tomato paste (see Tip, page 111)	1 tbsp.	15 mL
Frozen seafood mix, thawed	2 cups	500 mL
Chopped seeded tomato	1 cup	250 mL
Grated Parmesan cheese	1/4 cup	60 mL
Chopped fresh parsley	3 tbsp.	50 mL
(or 1 1/2 tsp., 7 mL, flakes)		
Lemon juice	2 tbsp.	30 mL

Combine first 8 ingredients in greased shallow 2 quart (2 L) casserole.

Whisk next 3 ingredients in small saucepan. Cook on medium for about 5 minutes, stirring occasionally, until hot, but not boiling. Add to rice mixture. Stir. Bake, covered, in 400°F (205°C) oven for about 35 minutes until rice is tender.

Add remaining 5 ingredients. Stir. Bake, covered, for about 10 minutes until seafood is cooked. Makes about 8 cups (2 L).

1 cup (250 mL): 160 Calories; 3.0 g Total Fat (0.5 g Mono, 0.5 g Poly, 1.0 g Sat); 3 mg Cholesterol; 27 g Carbohydrate; 1 g Fibre; 6 g Protein; 350 mg Sodium

Phyllo-Topped Fish Stew

A crisp, ruffled top makes this fish stew attractive and interesting—perfect for serving company. Mild and delicate flavours pair perfectly with fresh dill.

Butter (or hard margarine)	2 tbsp.	30 mL
Chopped celery	1/2 cup	125 mL
Chopped onion	1/2 cup	125 mL
Finely chopped carrot	1/2 cup	125 mL
All-purpose flour	3 tbsp.	50 mL
Prepared chicken broth	1 cup	250 mL
Milk	1 cup	250 mL
Reserved liquid from clams	2/3 cup	150 mL
Haddock fillets, any small bones removed, cut into 1 inch (2.5 cm) pieces	1 lb.	454 g
Frozen peas	1 cup	250 mL
Can of whole baby clams, drained and liquid reserved	5 oz.	142 g
Chopped fresh dill (or 3/4 tsp., 4 mL, dried)	1 tbsp.	15 mL
Phyllo pastry sheets, thawed according to package directions	6	6
Butter (or hard margarine), melted	3 tbsp.	50 mL

Melt first amount of butter in large saucepan on medium. Add next 3 ingredients. Cook for about 8 minutes, stirring often, until onion and celery are softened.

Add flour. Heat and stir for 1 minute. Slowly add broth, stirring constantly until smooth. Add milk and clam liquid. Heat and stir until boiling and thickened.

Add next 4 ingredients. Cook for about 4 minutes, stirring occasionally, until heated through. Transfer to greased shallow 2 quart (2 L) casserole.

Place 1 pastry sheet on work surface. Cover remaining sheets with damp towel to prevent drying. Brush sheet with second amount of butter. Bunch up loosely. Place over fish mixture. Repeat with remaining pastry sheets and butter. Bake, uncovered, in 375°F (190°C) oven for about 25 minutes until pastry is golden and fish flakes easily when tested with fork. Serves 6.

1 serving: 290 Calories; 12.0 g Total Fat (3.0 g Mono, 1.0 g Poly, 7.0 g Sat); 85 mg Cholesterol; 22 g Carbohydrate; 2 g Fibre; 24 g Protein; 440 mg Sodium

Seafood Chowder Casserole

Everyone's favourite hearty chowder flavours—served in casserole form!
Tender potatoes, creamy sauce and plenty of clams make this the perfect
all-in-one meal.

Butter (or hard margarine)	1 tsp.	5 mL
Diced peeled potato (1/2 inch, 12 mm, pieces)	4 cups	1 L
Chopped onion	1 1/2 cups	375 mL
Diced celery	1 cup	250 mL
Bacon slices, chopped	3	3
All-purpose flour	1/4 cup	60 mL
Salt	1/2 tsp.	2 mL
Pepper	1/4 tsp.	1 mL
Milk	1 1/2 cups	375 mL
Reserved liquid from clams	1/2 cup	125 mL
Halibut fillets, any small bones removed, cut into 3/4 inch (2 cm) pieces	3/4 lb.	340 g
Can of whole baby clams, drained and liquid reserved	5 oz.	142 g
Crushed round butter-flavoured crackers (about 9 crackers)	1/3 cup	75 mL
Chopped fresh parsley (or 3/4 tsp., 4 mL, flakes)	1 tbsp.	15 mL
Butter (or hard margarine), melted	1 tsp.	5 mL

Melt first amount of butter in Dutch oven on medium. Add next 4 ingredients. Cook for about 12 minutes, stirring often, until celery is softened.

Add next 3 ingredients. Heat and stir for 1 minute. Slowly add milk and clam liquid, stirring constantly until smooth. Heat and stir until boiling and thickened. Remove from heat.

Add fish and clams. Stir. Transfer to greased 3 quart (3 L) casserole. Bake, covered, in 400°F (205°C) oven for about 40 minutes, stirring at halftime, until potato is tender.

Combine remaining 3 ingredients in small bowl. Sprinkle over top. Bake, uncovered, for about 5 minutes until golden. Serves 6.

1 serving: 380 Calories; 20.0 g Total Fat (10.0 g Mono, 4.5 g Poly, 8.0 g Sat); 35 mg Cholesterol; 33 g Carbohydrate; 2 g Fibre; 19 g Protein; 550 mg Sodium

Salmon Soufflé Casserole

Elegant and appetizing, this golden soufflé has rich salmon flavour and a secret ingredient—spaghetti squash! Remember that soufflés should always be served immediately after baking.

Fine dry bread crumbs	1/4 cup	60 mL
Spaghetti squash	2 lbs.	900 g
Water	2 tbsp.	30 mL
Butter (or hard margarine)	1/3 cup	75 mL
All-purpose flour	1/3 cup	75 mL
Milk	2/3 cup	150 mL
Can of red salmon, drained, skin and round bones removed	7 1/2 oz.	213 g
Grated Parmesan cheese	1/2 cup	125 mL
Finely chopped green onion	2 tbsp.	30 mL
Egg whites (large), room temperature	6	6
Egg yolks (large)	6	6

Preheat oven to 350°F (175°C), see Note. Sprinkle greased 3 quart (3 L) casserole with bread crumbs until bottom and sides are coated. Set aside.

Cut squash in half lengthwise. Remove seeds. Place, cut-side down, in large microwave-safe bowl. Add water. Microwave, covered, on high for about 15 minutes until tender (see Tip, page 21). Drain. Shred squash pulp with fork. Transfer 1 cup (250 mL) to medium bowl. Reserve remainder for another use. Separate into strands. Discard shells.

Melt butter in medium saucepan on medium. Add flour. Heat and stir for 1 minute. Slowly add milk, stirring constantly until thickened. Remove from heat.

Add next 3 ingredients. Stir. Add to squash. Stir.

Beat egg whites in separate medium bowl until stiff peaks form. Beat egg yolks with same beaters in small bowl until frothy. Fold into squash mixture. Fold in egg whites until just combined. Carefully pour into prepared dish. Bake, uncovered, for about 45 minutes, without opening door, until puffed and golden. Serve immediately. Serves 6.

1 serving: 280 Calories; 18.0 g Total Fat (4.5 g Mono, 1.0 g Poly, 10.0 g Sat); 185 mg Cholesterol; 12 g Carbohydrate; trace Fibre; 17 g Protein; 480 mg Sodium

(continued on next page)

Note: A preheated oven contributes to a soufflé rising successfully. Once the soufflé is prepared, immediately place it in preheated oven to help preserve its "breath." Do not open the door while the soufflé is baking.

Baked Cioppino

This saucy seafood dish has plenty of haddock, chunky vegetables and a hint of white wine. Cioppino (pronounced chuh-PEE-noh) is great served with fresh crusty bread for dipping. You may substitute broth for wine if you prefer.

Cooking oil	2 tsp.	10 mL
Chopped peeled potato	2 cups	500 mL
Halved fresh white mushrooms	2 cups	500 mL
Chopped onion	1 cup	250 mL
Dried basil	1/2 tsp.	2 mL
Dried oregano	1/2 tsp.	2 mL
Garlic cloves, minced	2	2
(or 1/2 tsp., 2 mL, powder)		
Dry (or alcohol-free) white wine	1/2 cup	125 mL
Can of diced tomatoes, drained	14 oz.	398 mL
Prepared chicken broth	3/4 cup	175 mL
Tomato paste (see Tip, page 111)	1 tbsp.	15 mL
Granulated sugar	1/4 tsp.	1 mL
Salt	1/4 tsp.	1 mL
Pepper	1/4 tsp.	1 mL
Haddock fillets, any small bones removed, cut into 2 inch (5 cm) pieces	1 lb.	454 g

Heat cooking oil in large frying pan on medium. Add next 6 ingredients. Cook for about 10 minutes, stirring often, until onion is softened.

Add wine. Heat and stir for 2 minutes. Transfer to ungreased 2 quart (2 L) casserole.

Add next 6 ingredients. Stir. Cook, covered, in 375°F (190°C) oven for about 45 minutes until potato is tender.

Add fish. Stir. Cook, covered, for about 15 minutes until fish flakes easily when tested with fork. Makes about 7 cups (1.75 L).

1 cup (250 mL): 140 Calories; 2.0 g Total Fat (0 g Mono, 1.0 g Poly, 0 g Sat); 35 mg Cholesterol; 14 g Carbohydrate; 2 g Fibre; 15 g Protein; 330 mg Sodium

Seafood Shells in Rosé Sauce

Stuffed pasta shells always make for an elegant main course. These have a deliciously rich and lemony filling of seafood and cheese, surrounded by creamy tomato sauce.

Water	12 cups	3 L
Salt	1 1/2 tsp.	7 mL
Jumbo shell pasta	24	24
Tomato pasta sauce	2 cups	500 mL
Half-and-half cream	1/2 cup	125 mL
Cooking oil	1 tsp.	5 mL
Uncooked shrimp (peeled and deveined), chopped	3/4 lb.	340 g
Small bay scallops	1/2 lb.	225 g
Garlic cloves, minced (or 1/2 tsp., 2 mL, powder)	2	2
Salt	1/8 tsp.	0.5 mL
Pepper	1/4 tsp.	1 mL
Ricotta cheese	1 1/2 cups	375 mL
Lemon juice	2 tbsp.	30 mL
Grated lemon zest (see Tip, page 150)	1/4 tsp.	1 mL
Grated Parmesan cheese	1/3 cup	75 mL

Grated lemon zest, for garnish

Combine water and salt in Dutch oven. Bring to a boil. Add pasta shells. Boil, uncovered, for 10 to 12 minutes, stirring occasionally, until tender but firm. Drain. Rinse with cold water. Drain well.

Combine pasta sauce and cream in small bowl. Spread 1 cup (250 mL) in greased 9 x 13 inch (23 x 33 cm) baking dish.

Heat cooking oil in large frying pan on medium. Add next 5 ingredients. Cook for about 5 minutes, stirring occasionally, until shrimp start to turn pink. Transfer with slotted spoon to medium bowl. Discard remaining liquid.

Add next 3 ingredients to shrimp mixture. Stir. Fill pasta shells with shrimp mixture. Arrange over sauce mixture in baking dish. Pour remaining pasta sauce mixture over top.

(continued on next page)

Sprinkle with Parmesan cheese. Bake, covered, in 350°F (175°C) oven for 20 minutes. Remove cover. Bake for about 20 minutes until heated through.

Garnish with lemon zest. Makes 24 stuffed shells. Serves 6.

1 serving: 420 Calories; 16.0 g Total Fat (4.0 g Mono, 1.0 g Poly, 8.0 g Sat); 140 mg Cholesterol; 35 g Carbohydrate; 3 g Fibre; 33 g Protein; 540 mg Sodium

Pictured on page 54.

Roasted Veggies and Salmon

Delicious roasted salmon on a bed of sweet, caramelized vegetables—each component has wonderful flavours, and they make an exceptional pairing.

Cooking oil	2 tbsp.	30 mL
Garlic clove, minced	1	1
(or 1/4 tsp., 1 mL, powder)		
Salt	1/4 tsp.	1 mL
Dried crushed chilies	1/8 tsp.	0.5 mL
Medium fennel bulbs (white part only), cut into 8 wedges each	2	2
Baby carrots, halved lengthwise	2 cups	500 mL
Medium onion, cut into 8 wedges	1	1
Medium red pepper, cut into 8 wedges	1	1
Balsamic vinegar	2 tbsp.	30 mL
Salmon fillet, skin and any small bones removed	1 1/2 lbs.	680 g
Chopped fresh parsley	1 tbsp.	15 mL

Combine first 4 ingredients in large bowl. Reserve 1 tbsp. (15 mL) in small cup.

Add next 5 ingredients to remaining cooking oil mixture. Toss until coated. Arrange in single layer in ungreased large roasting pan. Cook, uncovered, in 450°F (230°C) oven for 30 minutes. Remove from oven. Stir.

Place fillet over vegetables. Brush with reserved cooking oil mixture. Cook, covered, for about 25 minutes until fish flakes easily when tested with fork.

Sprinkle with parsley. Serves 6.

1 serving: 273 Calories; 12.0 g Total Fat (3.5 g Mono, 6.0 g Poly, 2.0 g Sat); 62 mg Cholesterol; 17 g Carbohydrate; 4 g Fibre; 25 g Protein; 201 mg Sodium

Tuna Casserole

Always a hit with the kids! This is a bit of a twist on the traditional tuna casserole, with a crispy cornflake topping and lots of veggies added to make a balanced meal.

Water	8 cups	2 L
Salt	1 tsp.	5 mL
Rotini pasta	2 1/2 cups	625 mL
Cooking oil	2 tsp.	10 mL
Chopped fresh white mushrooms	1 cup	250 mL
Chopped onion	1 cup	250 mL
Finely chopped celery	1/2 cup	125 mL
Alfredo pasta sauce	1 1/4 cups	300 mL
Milk	3/4 cup	175 mL
Cans of flaked light tuna in water (6 oz., 170 g, each), drained	2	2
Frozen peas	1 cup	250 mL
Grated carrot	1/2 cup	125 mL
Grated havarti cheese	1/2 cup	125 mL
Coarsely ground pepper	1/4 tsp.	1 mL
Dried thyme	1/4 tsp.	1 mL
Grated lemon zest	1/4 tsp.	1 mL
Crushed cornflakes cereal	1/2 cup	125 mL
Butter (or hard margarine), melted	2 tbsp.	30 mL

Combine water and salt in large saucepan. Bring to a boil. Add pasta. Boil, uncovered, for 10 minutes, stirring occasionally. Drain. Transfer to large bowl.

Heat cooking oil in large frying pan on medium. Add next 3 ingredients. Cook for about 8 minutes, stirring often, until onion is softened.

Add pasta sauce and milk. Stir. Add to pasta.

Add next 7 ingredients. Stir. Transfer to greased 2 quart (2 L) casserole.

Combine cereal and butter in small bowl. Scatter over top. Bake, uncovered, in 350°F (175°C) oven for about 40 minutes until bubbling and golden. Serves 4.

1 serving: 620 Calories; 24.0 g Total Fat (2.5 g Mono, 2.0 g Poly, 13.0 g Sat); 85 mg Cholesterol; 61 g Carbohydrate; 4 g Fibre; 41 g Protein; 660 mg Sodium

Seafood Paella

A beautiful yellow paella (pronounced pi-AY-yuh) with sweet, tender seafood and a scattering of vegetables. A mild chili heat provides the perfect finishing touch.

Cooking oil	1 tbsp.	15 mL
Chopped onion	1 cup	250 mL
Garlic clove, minced	1	1
(or 1/4 tsp., 1 mL, powder)		
Converted white rice	1 1/2 cups	375 mL
Diced kielbasa (or other spiced cooked lean sausage)	1 cup	250 mL
Dry (or alcohol-free) white wine	1/2 cup	125 mL
Smoked (sweet) paprika	2 tsp.	10 mL
Chili paste (sambal oelek)	1 tsp.	5 mL
Turmeric	1/4 tsp.	1 mL
Boiling water	1 1/2 cups	375 mL
Prepared chicken broth	1 cup	250 mL
Uncooked medium shrimp (peeled and deveined)	1 lb.	454 g
Small bay scallops	3/4 lb.	340 g
Diced red pepper	1/2 cup	125 mL
Frozen peas	1/2 cup	125 mL

Heat cooking oil in large frying pan on medium. Add onion and garlic. Cook for about 5 minutes, stirring often, until onion is softened.

Add next 6 ingredients. Heat and stir for about 2 minutes until fragrant. Transfer to greased 3 quart (3 L) casserole.

Add boiling water and broth. Stir. Bake, covered, in 350°F (175°C) oven for 45 minutes.

Add remaining 4 ingredients. Stir. Bake, covered, for about 20 minutes, stirring at halftime, until rice is tender. Makes about 11 cups (2.75 L).

1 cup (250 mL): 230 Calories; 4.5 g Total Fat (1.5 g Mono, 1.5 g Poly, 1.0 g Sat); 80 mg Cholesterol; 25 g Carbohydrate; trace Fibre; 19 g Protein; 280 mg Sodium

Pictured on front cover.

Fish & Seafood

Picadillo Fish Casserole

A colourful mix of seafood and butternut squash with sweet, exotic flavours.
Perfect for serving over steamed rice.

Chopped butternut squash	4 cups	1 L
Can of diced tomatoes (with juice)	14 oz.	398 mL
Chopped onion	1 cup	250 mL
Sliced pimiento-stuffed olives	1/2 cup	125 mL
Can of diced green chilies	4 oz.	113 g
Chopped raisins	1/4 cup	60 mL
Chili powder	1 tbsp.	15 mL
Garlic clove, minced	1	1
(or 1/4 tsp., 1 mL, powder)		
Ground cinnamon	1/4 tsp.	1 mL
Tilapia fillets, any small bones removed, cut into 1 1/2 inch (3.8 cm) pieces	1 lb.	454 g
Uncooked medium shrimp (peeled and deveined)	1 lb.	454 g
Medium unsweetened coconut, toasted (see Tip, below)	1/4 cup	60 mL
Chopped fresh cilantro (or parsley)	2 tbsp.	30 mL

Combine first 9 ingredients in greased 9 x 13 inch (23 x 33 cm) baking dish. Cook, covered, in 375°F (190°C) oven for about 50 minutes until squash is tender.

Add fish and shrimp. Stir. Cook, uncovered, for about 15 minutes until shrimp turn pink and fish flakes easily when tested with fork.

Add coconut and cilantro. Stir gently. Makes about 11 cups (2.75 L).

1 cup (250 mL): 130 Calories; 3.5 g Total Fat (1.0 g Mono, 0 g Poly, 1.5 g Sat); 65 mg Cholesterol; 16 g Carbohydrate; 2 g Fibre; 11 g Protein; 360 mg Sodium

Pictured on page 89.

 tip
When toasting nuts, seeds or coconut, cooking times will vary for each type of nut—so never toast them together. For small amounts, place ingredient in an ungreased frying pan. Heat on medium for 3 to 5 minutes, stirring often, until golden. For larger amounts, spread ingredient evenly in an ungreased shallow pan. Bake in a 350°F (175°C) oven for 5 to 10 minutes, stirring or shaking often, until golden.

Pork Chop Scallop

Two popular favourites—pork chops and scalloped potatoes—in one creamy dish. Sure to be a hit with kids and grown-ups alike!

Thinly sliced unpeeled potato (see Note)	6 cups	1.5 L
Butter (or hard margarine)	1/4 cup	60 mL
Sliced fresh white mushrooms	1 1/2 cups	375 mL
Chopped onion	1 cup	250 mL
All-purpose flour	1/4 cup	60 mL
Dried thyme	1/4 tsp.	1 mL
Salt	1/2 tsp.	2 mL
Pepper	1/4 tsp.	1 mL
Milk	1 1/2 cups	375 mL
Cooking oil	1 tsp.	5 mL
Bone-in pork chops, trimmed of fat	6	6
Salt, sprinkle		
Pepper, sprinkle		

Arrange potato in greased 4 quart (4 L) casserole.

Melt butter in large saucepan on medium. Add mushrooms and onion. Cook for about 5 minutes, stirring often, until onion is softened.

Add next 4 ingredients. Heat and stir for 1 minute.

Slowly add milk, stirring constantly until smooth. Heat and stir until boiling and thickened. Pour over potato. Stir until coated. Spread evenly. Bake, covered, in 350°F (175°C) oven for 1 hour.

Heat cooking oil in large frying pan on medium-high. Sprinkle chops with salt and pepper. Cook chops, in 2 batches, for about 2 minutes per side, until browned. Arrange over potato mixture. Bake, covered, for about 20 minutes until potato is tender and internal temperature of pork reaches 160°F (71°C). Let stand, uncovered, for 10 minutes. Serves 6.

1 serving: 391 Calories; 14.0 g Total Fat (4.5 g Mono, 1.0 g Poly, 7.0 g Sat); 85 mg Cholesterol; 37 g Carbohydrate; 3 g Fibre; 29 g Protein; 330 mg Sodium

Note: Evenly sliced potatoes are one of the secrets to a good scallop. Use a mandoline slicer or food processor to ensure equal thickness.

Slow-Roasted Ribs

Ribs are always a crowd-pleaser! These are tender and tasty with a mixture of savoury spices and just a bit of sweetness.

Brown sugar, packed	1 tbsp.	15 mL
Dry mustard	1 tbsp.	15 mL
Garlic powder	1 tbsp.	15 mL
Onion powder	1 tbsp.	15 mL
Salt	1 1/2 tsp.	7 mL
Coarsely ground pepper	2 tsp.	10 mL
Paprika	2 tsp.	10 mL
Dried oregano	1 tsp.	5 mL
Dried thyme	1 tsp.	5 mL
Cayenne pepper	1/4 tsp.	1 mL
Pork side ribs, trimmed of fat and cut into 3-bone portions	5 lbs.	2.3 kg
Barbecue sauce	1/3 cup	75 mL

Combine first 10 ingredients in small bowl.

Rub over ribs. Arrange in large roasting pan. Cook, covered, in 250°F (120°C) oven for about 3 hours, turning at halftime, until meat is tender and starts to pull away from bones. Transfer ribs to large plate. Discard drippings.

Brush ribs with barbecue sauce. Return to roasting pan. Cook, uncovered, for about 30 minutes until glazed. Makes about 14 three-bone portions.

3-bone portion: 377 Calories; 16.0 g Total Fat (7.0 g Mono, 1.0 g Poly, 6.0 g Sat); 131 mg Cholesterol; 4 g Carbohydrate; 0 g Fibre; 50 g Protein; 420 mg Sodium

Pictured on page 126.

1. Picadillo Fish Casserole, page 86
2. Huevos Rancheros Casserole, page 22

88   Pork & Lamb

One-Pot Rice and Chops

This family-friendly meal of dilly pork chops with rice and carrots is loaded with flavour. Use thicker chops if you want them to be more tender.

Dried dillweed	1 1/2 tsp.	7 mL
Garlic powder	1/2 tsp.	2 mL
Salt	1/4 tsp.	1 mL
Pepper	1/2 tsp.	2 mL
Bone-in pork chops, trimmed of fat	4	4
Cooking oil	2 tsp.	10 mL
Prepared chicken broth	2 cups	500 mL
Diced carrot	1 1/2 cups	375 mL
Long-grain white rice	1 1/4 cups	300 mL
Water	1 cup	250 mL

Combine first 4 ingredients in small cup. Sprinkle half over both sides of chops. Set aside remaining seasoning mixture.

Heat cooking oil in Dutch oven on medium-high. Add chops. Cook for about 2 minutes per side until browned. Transfer to plate.

Add remaining 4 ingredients and remaining dillweed mixture to same pot. Stir. Bring to a boil. Remove from heat. Carefully arrange chops over top. Cook, covered, in 350°F (175°C) oven for about 30 minutes until pork is no longer pink inside and rice is almost tender. Let stand, covered, for about 10 minutes until rice is tender. Serves 4.

1 serving: 369 Calories; 4.5 g Total Fat (1.5 g Mono, 1.5 g Poly, 1.0 g Sat); 51 mg Cholesterol; 53 g Carbohydrate; 2 g Fibre; 28 g Protein; 467 mg Sodium

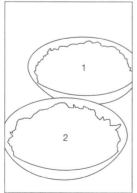

1. Fruity Lamb Tagine, page 93
2. Spiced Meatballs and Rice, page 92

Spiced Meatballs and Rice

Tasty lamb meatballs in an attractive rice casserole. This dish is rich and filling, with tomato and parsley adding a nice freshness.

Large egg, fork-beaten	1	1
Fine dry bread crumbs	1/4 cup	60 mL
Finely chopped onion	1/4 cup	60 mL
Dried mint leaves	1/2 tsp.	2 mL
Salt	1/2 tsp.	2 mL
Pepper	1/2 tsp.	2 mL
Ground cinnamon	1/4 tsp.	1 mL
Ground cloves	1/8 tsp.	0.5 mL
Ground nutmeg	1/8 tsp.	0.5 mL
Lean ground lamb	1 lb.	454 g
Long-grain white rice	1 cup	250 mL
Prepared chicken broth	2 cups	500 mL
Chopped seeded tomato	1/4 cup	60 mL
Chopped fresh parsley	2 tbsp.	30 mL
Slivered almonds, toasted (see Tip, page 86)	2 tbsp.	30 mL

Combine first 9 ingredients in large bowl.

Add lamb. Mix well. Roll into balls, using 1 tbsp. (15 mL) for each. Makes about 26 meatballs.

Spread rice evenly in greased shallow 2 quart (2 L) casserole. Arrange meatballs over rice.

Pour broth over top. Bake, covered, in 375°F (190°C) oven for about 55 minutes until rice is tender and meatballs are no longer pink inside. Let stand, covered, for 10 minutes.

Scatter remaining 3 ingredients over top. Serves 4.

1 serving: 563 Calories; 25.0 g Total Fat (11.0 g Mono, 2.5 g Poly, 10.0 g Sat); 145 mg Cholesterol; 46 g Carbohydrate; 1 g Fibre; 36 g Protein; 533 mg Sodium

Pictured on page 90.

Fruity Lamb Tagine

Sweet lamb stew that's saucy enough to serve over couscous or brown basmati rice. Freeze leftovers in individual portions and reheat on the stovetop or in the microwave.

All-purpose flour	2 tbsp.	30 mL
Salt	1/4 tsp.	1 mL
Pepper	1/4 tsp.	1 mL
Boneless lamb shoulder, trimmed of fat and cut into 1 inch (2.5 cm) pieces	1 1/2 lbs.	680 g
Cooking oil	2 tsp.	10 mL
Coarsely chopped onion	1 1/2 cups	375 mL
Ground coriander	1 tsp.	5 mL
Ground cumin	1 tsp.	5 mL
Garlic cloves, minced (or 1/2 tsp., 2 mL, powder)	2	2
Ground cinnamon	1/2 tsp.	2 mL
Cayenne pepper	1/8 tsp.	0.5 mL
Can of diced tomatoes (with juice)	14 oz.	398 mL
Prepared chicken broth	1 1/4 cups	300 mL
Coarsely chopped dried apricot	1/2 cup	125 mL
Coarsely chopped pitted dates	1/2 cup	125 mL
Sliced natural almonds, toasted (see Tip, page 86)	1/4 cup	60 mL

Combine first 3 ingredients in large resealable freezer bag. Add lamb. Seal bag. Toss until coated. Transfer lamb to greased 2 quart (2 L) casserole.

Heat cooking oil in large frying pan on medium. Add next 6 ingredients. Cook for about 5 minutes, stirring often, until onion starts to soften.

Add tomatoes and broth. Heat and stir, scraping any brown bits from bottom of pan, until boiling. Add to lamb.

Add apricot and dates. Stir. Cook, covered, in 325°F (160°C) oven for about 90 minutes until lamb is tender.

Scatter almonds over top. Makes about 8 cups (2 L).

1 cup (250 mL): 236 Calories; 9.0 g Total Fat (4.5 g Mono, 1.5 g Poly, 2.5 g Sat); 57 mg Cholesterol; 20 g Carbohydrate; 3 g Fibre; 19 g Protein; 325 mg Sodium

Pictured on page 90.

Stout Lamb Stew

A rich-flavoured stew with tender lamb balanced by a dark sauce containing stout beer. The combination of ingredients creates a satisfying and complete meal. Serve with biscuits.

All-purpose flour	1/4 cup	60 mL
Seasoned salt	1 tsp.	5 mL
Pepper	1/2 tsp.	2 mL
Stewing lamb, trimmed of fat	1 1/2 lbs.	680 g
Chopped peeled potato	2 cups	500 mL
Chopped yellow turnip (rutabaga)	2 cups	500 mL
Sliced fresh white mushrooms	2 cups	500 mL
Sliced onion	1 cup	250 mL
Bay leaves	2	2
Stout beer	1 1/3 cups	325 mL
Prepared beef broth	1 cup	250 mL
Tomato paste (see Tip, page 111)	2 tbsp.	30 mL
Garlic cloves, minced (or 1/2 tsp., 2 mL, powder)	2	2
Balsamic vinegar	1 tbsp.	15 mL

Combine first 3 ingredients in large resealable freezer bag. Add lamb. Seal bag. Toss until coated. Transfer lamb to greased 4 quart (4 L) casserole. Reserve remaining flour mixture.

Scatter next 5 ingredients over lamb.

Whisk next 4 ingredients and reserved flour mixture in medium bowl. Pour over vegetables. Stir. Cook, covered, in 350°F (175°C) oven for about 2 hours until lamb and vegetables are tender. Remove and discard bay leaves.

Add vinegar. Stir. Makes about 8 cups (2 L).

1 cup (250 mL): 342 Calories; 23.0 g Total Fat (7.0 g Mono, 1.0 g Poly, 11.0 g Sat); 68 mg Cholesterol; 17 g Carbohydrate; 2 g Fibre; 17 g Protein; 334 mg Sodium

Pictured on page 53.

 tip To make soured milk, measure 1 tbsp. (15 mL) white vinegar or lemon juice into a 1 cup (250 mL) liquid measure. Add enough milk to make 1 cup (250 mL). Stir. Let stand for 1 minute.

Pork Sage Dumpling Stew

A complete meal of savoury pork and sweet potato stew topped with sage-speckled dumplings—makes a great family meal for chilly autumn days.

All-purpose flour	3 tbsp.	50 mL
Salt	1/4 tsp.	1 mL
Pepper	1/4 tsp.	1 mL
Boneless pork shoulder blade steak, trimmed of fat and cut into 1 inch (2.5 cm) pieces	1 lb.	454 g
Chopped onion	1 1/2 cups	375 mL
Cubed peeled orange-fleshed sweet potato	1 1/2 cups	375 mL
Chopped celery	1 cup	250 mL
Dried marjoram	1/2 tsp.	2 mL
Dried sage	1/2 tsp.	2 mL
Prepared chicken broth	1 1/2 cups	375 mL
Biscuit mix	1 cup	250 mL
Dried sage	1/4 tsp.	1 mL
Buttermilk (or soured milk, see Tip, page 94)	1/2 cup	125 mL

Combine first 3 ingredients in large resealable freezer bag. Add pork. Seal bag. Toss until coated. Transfer pork to greased 3 quart (3 L) casserole. Reserve remaining flour mixture.

Scatter next 5 ingredients over pork.

Whisk broth and reserved flour mixture in medium bowl. Pour over vegetables. Stir. Bake, covered, in 350°F (175°C) oven for about 90 minutes until pork is tender. Stir.

Combine biscuit mix and sage in small bowl. Make a well in centre.

Add buttermilk to well. Stir until just moistened. Drop batter onto hot pork mixture in 8 mounds, using about 2 tbsp. (30 mL) for each. Bake, covered, for about 20 minutes until wooden pick inserted in centre of dumpling comes out clean. Serves 4.

1 serving: 567 Calories; 26.0 g Total Fat (9.0 g Mono, 2.5 g Poly, 8.0 g Sat); 69 mg Cholesterol; 53 g Carbohydrate; 4 g Fibre; 28 g Protein; 1028 mg Sodium

Sweet Potato Pork

Colourfully topped with sweet potatoes, this casserole features ground pork and veggies with a gentle spiciness.

Cooking oil	1 tsp.	5 mL
Lean ground pork	1 lb.	454 g
Chopped carrot	1 cup	250 mL
Chopped onion	3/4 cup	175 mL
All-purpose flour	1 tbsp.	15 mL
Dried oregano	1/2 tsp.	2 mL
Ground cumin	1/2 tsp.	2 mL
Ground cinnamon	1/4 tsp.	1 mL
Ground allspice	1/8 tsp.	0.5 mL
Salt	1/8 tsp.	0.5 mL
Pepper	1/8 tsp.	0.5 mL
Prepared chicken broth	1/2 cup	125 mL
Chopped cauliflower	1 cup	250 mL
Chopped red pepper	1/2 cup	125 mL
Lime juice	2 tbsp.	30 mL
Chili paste (sambal oelek)	1 tsp.	5 mL
Garlic clove, minced	1	1
(or 1/4 tsp., 1 mL, powder)		
Mashed orange-fleshed sweet potato	3 cups	750 mL
(about 1 1/2 lbs., 680 g, uncooked), see Note		
Butter (or hard margarine), melted	1 tbsp.	15 mL
Salt	1/8 tsp.	0.5 mL
Pepper	1/4 tsp.	1 mL

Heat cooking oil in large frying pan on medium-high. Add next 3 ingredients. Scramble-fry for about 5 minutes until pork is no longer pink. Drain.

Add next 7 ingredients. Heat and stir for 1 minute. Add broth. Heat and stir until thickened.

Add next 5 ingredients. Stir. Transfer to greased 8 x 8 inch (20 x 20 cm) baking dish.

(continued on next page)

96

Combine remaining 4 ingredients in medium bowl. Spread over top. Bake in 350°F (175°C) oven for about 1 hour until filling is bubbling. Serves 4.

1 serving: 532 Calories; 29.0 g Total Fat (12.0 g Mono, 12.5 g Poly, 11.0 g Sat); 90 mg Cholesterol; 45 g Carbohydrate; 7 g Fibre; 24 g Protein; 375 mg Sodium

Note: You can use canned sweet potato, mashed until smooth. If you have fresh orange-fleshed sweet potato on hand, just microwave until soft, then peel and mash.

Oven Pork Stir-Fry

Stir-fry flavours without the frying! This dish can be made even easier by using pre-cut stir-fry vegetables. Prepare some rice on the stovetop while this cooks in the oven and dinner is ready to go!

Pork tenderloin, trimmed of fat, halved lengthwise and cut crosswise into 1/2 inch (12 mm) slices	1 lb.	454 g
Baby carrots, halved lengthwise	1 cup	250 mL
Diagonally sliced celery (1/2 inch, 12 mm, slices)	1 cup	250 mL
Chopped red pepper (1 1/2 inch, 3.8 cm, pieces)	3/4 cup	175 mL
Chopped yellow pepper (1 1/2 inch, 3.8 cm, pieces)	3/4 cup	175 mL
Sliced onion (1/2 inch, 12 mm, slices)	3/4 cup	175 mL
Prepared vegetable broth	1/4 cup	60 mL
Sweet chili sauce	1/4 cup	60 mL
All-purpose flour	1 tbsp.	15 mL
Soy sauce	1 tbsp.	15 mL
Finely grated ginger root (or 1/2 tsp., 2 mL, ground ginger)	2 tsp.	10 mL
Garlic clove, minced (or 1/4 tsp., 1 mL, powder)	1	1

Combine first 6 ingredients in greased 9 x 13 inch (23 x 33 cm) baking dish.

Combine remaining 6 ingredients in small bowl. Add to pork mixture. Stir. Cook, covered, in 375°F (190°C) oven for about 40 minutes until vegetables are tender-crisp and pork is no longer pink inside. Makes about 6 cups (1.5 L).

1 cup (250 mL): 198 Calories; 9.0 g Total Fat (4.0 g Mono, 1.0 g Poly, 3.0 g Sat); 45 mg Cholesterol; 12 g Carbohydrate; 1 g Fibre; 17 g Protein; 311 mg Sodium

Bavarian Pork Casserole

Saucy cabbage and pork with sweetness from apple—all wonderfully seasoned with spices, beer and apple cider vinegar. Serve with mashed or boiled potatoes.

Bacon slices, chopped	2	2
Shredded green cabbage, lightly packed	2 cups	500 mL
Sliced onion	1 cup	250 mL
Sliced peeled cooking apple (such as McIntosh)	1 cup	250 mL
Caraway seed	1/2 tsp.	2 mL
Salt	1/4 tsp.	1 mL
Pepper	1/8 tsp.	0.5 mL
Beer	2/3 cup	150 mL
All-purpose flour	1 tbsp.	15 mL
Brown sugar, packed	1 tbsp.	15 mL
Apple cider vinegar	2 tsp.	10 mL
Dijon mustard	2 tsp.	10 mL
Boneless pork shoulder blade steak, trimmed of fat and cut into 3/4 inch (2 cm) pieces	1 lb.	454 g
Sour cream	1/4 cup	60 mL
Chopped fresh parsley (or 1/2 tsp., 2 mL, flakes)	2 tsp.	10 mL

Cook bacon in large frying pan on medium until crisp. Transfer with slotted spoon to paper towel-lined plate to drain. Discard all but 2 tsp. (10 mL) drippings from pan.

Add next 6 ingredients to same frying pan. Cook for about 10 minutes, stirring often, until onion is softened. Remove from heat.

Whisk next 5 ingredients in small bowl. Add to cabbage mixture. Add bacon. Stir.

Arrange pork in greased shallow 2 quart (2 L) casserole. Spoon cabbage mixture over top. Cook, covered, in 350°F (175°C) oven for about 40 minutes until cabbage is tender and pork is no longer pink inside.

(continued on next page)

98

Add sour cream. Stir.

Sprinkle with parsley. Makes about 5 cups (1.25 L).

1 cup (250 mL): 312 Calories; 15.0 g Total Fat (6.0 g Mono, 1.5 g Poly, 6.0 g Sat); 90 mg Cholesterol; 12 g Carbohydrate; 1 g Fibre; 29 g Protein; 314 mg Sodium

Chorizo Lentil Casserole

An earthy blend of dark lentils, spicy sausage and carrots with a golden topping.

Cooking oil	2 tsp.	10 mL
Chorizo (or hot Italian) sausage, cut into 1/2 inch (12 mm) pieces	3/4 lb.	340 g
Chopped onion	1 cup	250 mL
Prepared chicken broth	1 3/4 cups	425 mL
Dried green lentils	1 cup	250 mL
Sliced carrot	1 cup	250 mL
Italian seasoning	1/2 tsp.	2 mL
Fine dry bread crumbs	1/2 cup	125 mL
Grated Parmesan cheese	2 tbsp.	30 mL
Cooking oil	1 tbsp.	15 mL
Chopped fresh basil (or 1/4 tsp., 1 mL, dried)	1 tsp.	5 mL

Heat cooking oil in large frying pan on medium-high. Add sausage and onion. Cook for about 5 minutes, stirring often, until sausage is browned and onion is softened.

Add broth. Heat and stir, scraping any brown bits from bottom of pan, until boiling.

Add next 3 ingredients. Stir. Transfer to greased 2 quart (2 L) casserole. Bake, covered, in 350°F (175°C) oven for about 55 minutes, stirring at halftime, until lentils are tender and liquid is absorbed.

Combine remaining 4 ingredients in small bowl. Sprinkle over top. Broil on centre rack in oven for about 2 minutes until golden. Serves 4.

1 serving: 615 Calories; 31.0 g Total Fat (12.0 g Mono, 7.0 g Poly, 10.0 g Sat); 51 mg Cholesterol; 46 g Carbohydrate; 7 g Fibre; 35 g Protein; 927 mg Sodium

Lamb Lentil Casserole

Dark lentils and lamb served with sweet and tangy caramelized onions. This warmly spiced and satisfying combination goes great with rice pilaf or couscous.

Cooking oil	1 tsp.	5 mL
Lean ground lamb	1 lb.	454 g
Ground allspice	1/2 tsp.	2 mL
Ground coriander	1/2 tsp.	2 mL
Chili powder	1/4 tsp.	1 mL
Salt	1/4 tsp.	1 mL
Pepper	1/4 tsp.	1 mL
Dried green lentils	1 cup	250 mL
Prepared beef broth	1 cup	250 mL
Water	3/4 cup	175 mL
Bay leaf	1	1
Cooking oil	1 tbsp.	15 mL
Thinly sliced onion	3 cups	750 mL
Brown sugar, packed	2 tbsp.	30 mL
Red wine vinegar	1 tbsp.	15 mL
Chopped fresh parsley	2 tbsp.	30 mL

Heat first amount of cooking oil in large frying pan on medium-high. Add next 6 ingredients. Scramble-fry for about 8 minutes until lamb is browned. Drain.

Add next 4 ingredients. Stir. Bring to a boil. Transfer to greased 2 quart (2 L) casserole. Cook, covered, in 375°F (190°C) oven for about 40 minutes, stirring at halftime, until lentils are tender. Remove and discard bay leaf.

Heat second amount of cooking oil in same frying pan on medium. Add onion. Cook for about 20 minutes, stirring often, until caramelized.

Add brown sugar and vinegar. Heat and stir for 1 minute. Scatter over lentil mixture.

Sprinkle with parsley. Makes about 4 2/3 cups (1.15 L).

1 cup (250 mL): 510 Calories; 24.0 g Total Fat (9.0 g Mono, 4.0 g Poly, 9.0 g Sat); 94 mg Cholesterol; 37 g Carbohydrate; 6 g Fibre; 37 g Protein; 388 mg Sodium

Curried Lamb Shanks

Serve this casserole of extremely tender lamb over a bed of basmati rice. Tangy curry tomato sauce and a sprinkle of cilantro brighten the flavours.

Cooking oil	1 tsp.	5 mL
Lamb shanks (about 3 – 4 lbs., 1.4 – 1.8 kg), see Note	6	6
Salt	1/4 tsp.	1 mL
Pepper	1/4 tsp.	1 mL
Chopped onion	1 cup	250 mL
Curry powder	2 tbsp.	30 mL
Garlic cloves, minced (or 1 tsp., 5 mL, powder)	4	4
Finely grated ginger root (or 3/4 tsp., 4 mL, ground ginger)	1 tbsp.	15 mL
Can of tomato sauce	25 oz.	680 mL
Water	2/3 cup	150 mL
Lemon juice	2 tbsp.	30 mL
Granulated sugar	1 tsp.	5 mL
Chopped fresh cilantro (or parsley)	1/4 cup	60 mL

Heat cooking oil in large frying pan on medium-high. Sprinkle lamb with salt and pepper. Cook lamb, in 2 batches, for about 10 minutes, until browned on all sides. Transfer to greased medium roasting pan. Reduce heat to medium.

Add next 4 ingredients to same frying pan. Cook for about 5 minutes, stirring often, until onion starts to brown.

Add next 4 ingredients. Heat and stir, scraping any brown bits from bottom of pan, until boiling. Pour over lamb. Cook, covered, in 350°F (175°C) oven for about 2 1/2 hours until lamb is tender. Skim and discard fat from sauce.

Sprinkle with cilantro. Serves 6.

1 serving: 470 Calories; 19.0 g Total Fat (8.0 g Mono, 3.0 g Poly, 5.0 g Sat); 145 mg Cholesterol; 27 g Carbohydrate; 5 g Fibre; 50 g Protein; 862 mg Sodium

Note: Lamb shanks are commonly found in frozen bulk packages. If using frozen shanks, remember to thaw them before using.

Sausage-Stuffed Cannelloni

A vibrantly flavoured cannelloni dish with spicy sausage, spinach and tangy tomato sauce. A sprinkle of goat cheese provides the perfect finishing touch.

Hot Italian sausage, casing removed	1/2 lb.	225 g
Chopped fresh white mushrooms	1 cup	250 mL
Chopped onion	1 cup	250 mL
Large egg, fork-beaten	1	1
2% cottage cheese	1 1/2 cups	375 mL
Box of frozen chopped spinach, thawed and squeezed dry	10 oz.	300 g
Tomato pasta sauce	2 3/4 cups	675 mL
Jar of roasted red peppers, drained	12 oz.	340 mL
Water	1/2 cup	125 mL
Cooking oil	2 tbsp.	30 mL
Garlic clove, chopped (or 1/4 tsp., 1 mL, powder)	1	1
Salt	1/8 tsp.	0.5 mL
Pepper	1/4 tsp.	1 mL
Oven-ready cannelloni shells	18	18
Goat (chèvre) cheese, cut up	4 oz.	113 g
Dried oregano	1/4 tsp.	1 mL
Grated lemon zest	1/4 tsp.	1 mL

Scramble-fry first 3 ingredients in large frying pan on medium for about 8 minutes until sausage is no longer pink. Drain. Transfer to large bowl. Cool.

Add next 3 ingredients. Stir.

Process next 7 ingredients in blender until smooth. Spread 2 cups (500 mL) in greased 9 x 13 inch (23 x 33 cm) baking dish.

Fill pasta shells with sausage mixture. Arrange in single layer over sauce mixture in baking dish. Pour remaining sauce mixture over top. Bake, covered, in 350°F (175°C) oven for about 50 minutes until pasta is tender.

Combine remaining 3 ingredients in small cup. Sprinkle over top. Bake, uncovered, for about 5 minutes until cheese is softened. Let stand for 10 minutes. Makes 18 cannelloni.

(continued on next page)

Pork & Lamb

1 cannelloni: 165 Calories; 9.0 g Total Fat (3.0 g Mono, 1.0 g Poly, 3.5 g Sat); 19 mg Cholesterol; 12 g Carbohydrate; 2 g Fibre; 12 g Protein; 436 mg Sodium

Pictured on page 107.

Sausage Fennel Casserole

Rich, comforting flavours reminiscent of the cuisine of Southern France. Serve with a salad of baby greens and a full-bodied red wine.

Cans of navy (or white kidney) beans (19 oz., 540 mL, each), rinsed and drained	2	2
Chopped carrot	3 cups	750 mL
Chopped fennel bulb (white part only)	3 cups	750 mL
Chopped celery	1 cup	250 mL
Chopped onion	1 cup	250 mL
Fennel seed, crushed (see Tip, page 130)	1 tsp.	5 mL
Garlic cloves, minced (or 1/2 tsp., 2 mL, powder)	2	2
Salt	1/4 tsp.	1 mL
Pepper	1/4 tsp.	1 mL
Cooking oil	1 tsp.	5 mL
Italian sausage, cut into 1/2 inch (12 mm) pieces	3/4 lb.	340 g
Boneless, skinless chicken thighs, quartered	1/2 lb.	225 g
Chopped tomato	1 cup	250 mL
Chopped fresh parsley (or 2 tsp., 10 mL, flakes)	1/4 cup	60 mL

Combine first 9 ingredients in greased 4 quart (4 L) casserole.

Heat cooking oil in large frying pan on medium-high. Add sausage and chicken. Cook for about 5 minutes, stirring often, until chicken is browned. Transfer with slotted spoon to casserole. Discard drippings. Stir. Cook, covered, in 375°F (190°C) oven for about 75 minutes until vegetables are tender.

Add tomato and parsley. Stir. Makes about 13 cups (3.25 L).

1 cup (250 mL): 185 Calories; 9.0 g Total Fat (3.0 g Mono, 1.0 g Poly, 2.5 g Sat); 30 mg Cholesterol; 14 g Carbohydrate; 2 g Fibre; 13 g Protein; 400 mg Sodium

Pork Polenta Casserole

Herb-speckled pork stew topped with cheesy polenta slices. You'll find tasty bites of grape tomato hiding in the stew! A flavourful dish that makes a complete meal.

Cooking oil	1 tsp.	5 mL
Boneless pork shoulder blade steak, trimmed of fat and cut into 1 1/2 inch (3.8 cm) pieces	2 lbs.	900 g
Salt	1/4 tsp.	1 mL
Pepper	1/4 tsp.	1 mL
Cooking oil	1 tsp.	5 mL
Chopped carrot	2 cups	500 mL
Chopped onion	1 cup	250 mL
Garlic cloves, minced (or 1/2 tsp., 2 mL, powder)	2	2
All-purpose flour	2 tbsp.	30 mL
Prepared chicken broth	1 3/4 cups	425 mL
Chopped zucchini (with peel)	2 cups	500 mL
Grape tomatoes, halved	1 cup	250 mL
Chopped fresh basil (or 1 1/2 tsp., 7 mL, dried)	2 tbsp.	30 mL
Chopped fresh oregano (or 1/2 tsp., 2 mL, dried)	2 tsp.	10 mL
Polenta roll, cut into 24 slices	2.2 lbs.	1 kg
Grated Italian cheese blend	1 cup	250 mL

Heat first amount of cooking oil in large frying pan on medium-high. Sprinkle pork with salt and pepper. Cook pork, in 2 batches, for about 5 minutes, stirring occasionally, until browned. Transfer to greased 9 x 13 inch (23 x 33 cm) baking dish. Reduce heat to medium.

Heat second amount of cooking oil in same frying pan. Add next 3 ingredients. Cook for about 5 minutes, stirring often, until onion is softened.

Add flour. Heat and stir for 1 minute. Slowly add broth, stirring constantly until smooth. Heat and stir until boiling and thickened. Pour over pork. Bake, covered, in 350°F (175°C) oven for about 1 hour until pork is tender.

(continued on next page)

Add next 4 ingredients. Stir.

Arrange polenta slices in overlapping pattern over top. Sprinkle with cheese. Bake, uncovered, for about 40 minutes until cheese is melted. Let stand for 10 minutes. Serves 8.

1 serving: 457 Calories; 25.0 g Total Fat (10.0 g Mono, 3.0 g Poly, 9.0 g Sat); 77 mg Cholesterol; 28 g Carbohydrate; 3 g Fibre; 28 g Protein; 726 mg Sodium

Pictured on page 107.

Coconut Rice and Pork

A blend of subtle coconut-infused rice with brightly coloured vegetables and pork. A complete meal that the whole family is sure to enjoy.

Cooking oil	2 tsp.	10 mL
Boneless fast-fry pork chops, cut into 1/2 inch (12 mm) slices	1 lb.	454 g
Chopped onion	1/3 cup	75 mL
Lemon pepper	1/2 tsp.	2 mL
Sliced carrot	2 cups	500 mL
Can of coconut milk	14 oz.	398 mL
Converted white rice	1 cup	250 mL
Water	1/2 cup	125 mL
Grated lime zest	1 tsp.	5 mL
Salt	1/2 tsp.	2 mL
Dried crushed chilies	1/4 tsp.	1 mL
Frozen cut green beans	2 cups	500 mL

Heat cooking oil in large frying pan on medium-high. Add next 3 ingredients. Cook for about 3 minutes, stirring often, until pork is browned. Transfer to greased 9 x 13 inch (23 x 33 cm) baking dish.

Add next 7 ingredients. Stir. Bake, covered, in 375°F (190°C) oven for about 1 hour until rice is tender.

Add beans. Stir. Bake, covered, for about 15 minutes until beans are tender. Makes about 8 cups (2 L).

1 cup (250 mL): 290 Calories; 15.0 g Total Fat (2.0 g Mono, 1.0 g Poly, 10.0 g Sat); 30 mg Cholesterol; 25 g Carbohydrate; 2 g Fibre; 16 g Protein; 270 mg Sodium

Swiss Ham Bake

This tasty casserole will please even the pickiest of kids with its cheesy noodles, ham, and crisp crumb topping—it's simple yet satisfying.

Water	8 cups	2 L
Salt	1 tsp.	5 mL
Penne pasta	2 cups	500 mL
Milk	2 cups	500 mL
Diced cooked ham	1 1/2 cups	375 mL
Frozen cut green beans	1 1/2 cups	375 mL
Can of condensed cream of chicken soup	10 oz.	284 mL
Dijon mustard	1 tsp.	5 mL
Pepper	1/4 tsp.	1 mL
Fine dry bread crumbs	1/2 cup	125 mL
Grated Swiss cheese	1/4 cup	60 mL
Butter (or hard margarine), melted	2 tbsp.	30 mL

Combine water and salt in large saucepan. Bring to a boil. Add pasta. Boil, uncovered, for 14 to 16 minutes, stirring occasionally, until tender but firm. Drain. Return to same pot.

Add next 6 ingredients. Stir. Transfer to greased 9 x 13 inch (23 x 33 cm) baking dish.

Combine remaining 3 ingredients in small bowl. Sprinkle over top. Bake in 375°F (190°C) oven for about 30 minutes until bubbling and golden. Serves 6.

1 serving: 367 Calories; 16.0 g Total Fat (5.0 g Mono, 1.5 g Poly, 7.0 g Sat); 44 mg Cholesterol; 37 g Carbohydrate; 2 g Fibre; 18 g Protein; 868 mg Sodium

Pictured at right.

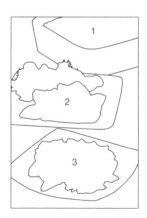

1. Pork Polenta Casserole, page 104
2. Sausage-Stuffed Cannelloni, page 102
3. Swiss Ham Bake, above

Pork & Lamb

Moroccan Veggie Casserole

This nutritious dish features mildly seasoned brown rice with sweet potato and veggies.

Chopped peeled orange-fleshed sweet potato	2 cups	500 mL
Prepared vegetable broth	2 cups	500 mL
Chopped onion	1 cup	250 mL
Chopped red pepper	1 cup	250 mL
Chopped zucchini (with peel), 1/2 inch (12 mm) pieces	1 cup	250 mL
Long-grain brown rice	1 cup	250 mL
Chopped tomato	1/2 cup	125 mL
Lemon juice	2 tbsp.	30 mL
Liquid honey	2 tsp.	10 mL
Ground cinnamon	1/4 tsp.	1 mL
Ground cumin	1/4 tsp.	1 mL
Ground ginger	1/4 tsp.	1 mL

Combine all 12 ingredients in greased 2 quart (2 L) casserole. Bake, covered, in 375°F (190°C) oven for about 75 minutes, stirring at halftime, until rice is tender. Let stand, covered, for about 10 minutes until liquid is absorbed. Makes about 7 cups (1.75 L).

1 cup (250 mL): 160 Calories; 1.0 g Total Fat (0 g Mono, 0 g Poly, 0 g Sat); 0 mg Cholesterol; 35 g Carbohydrate; 3 g Fibre; 3 g Protein; 296 mg Sodium

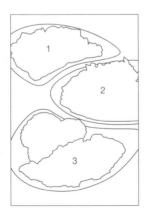

1. Potato Tot Shepherd's Pie, page 69
2. Taco Salad Casserole, page 43
3. Smoky Mac 'n' Cheese, page 113

Upside-Down Tamale Pie

Tasty tamale pie with spicy tomatoes and lentils over a thick cornmeal crust—the spice is nice, but you can use a milder salsa if you prefer.

Prepared vegetable broth	1 1/2 cups	375 mL
Water	1 1/2 cups	375 mL
Chili paste (sambal oelek)	1 tsp.	5 mL
Garlic clove, minced	1	1
(or 1/4 tsp., 1 mL, powder)		
Yellow cornmeal	1 cup	250 mL
Grated medium Cheddar cheese	1/2 cup	125 mL
Finely chopped green onion	2 tbsp.	30 mL
Butter (or hard margarine)	1 tbsp.	15 mL
Cooking oil	2 tsp.	10 mL
Chopped onion	1 cup	250 mL
Can of lentils, rinsed and drained	19 oz.	540 mL
Chopped green pepper	1/2 cup	125 mL
Hot salsa	1/2 cup	125 mL
Tomato paste (see Tip, page 111)	1 tbsp.	15 mL
Chili powder	2 tsp.	10 mL
Grated medium Cheddar cheese	1/2 cup	125 mL
Sliced black olives	2 tbsp.	30 mL

Combine first 4 ingredients in large saucepan. Bring to a boil. Reduce heat to medium. Slowly add cornmeal, stirring constantly. Heat and stir for about 5 minutes until mixture is thick. Remove from heat.

Add next 3 ingredients. Stir until cheese is melted. Transfer to greased 9 inch (23 cm) deep dish pie plate. Let stand for 5 minutes. Spread evenly in bottom and up sides of pie plate. Let stand for about 20 minutes until firm.

Heat cooking oil in large frying pan on medium. Add onion. Cook for about 5 minutes, stirring often, until softened.

Add next 5 ingredients. Stir. Spread over cornmeal mixture.

Sprinkle with second amount of cheese and olives. Bake in 350°F (175°C) oven for about 45 minutes until heated through. Let stand for 10 minutes. Cuts into 6 wedges.

1 wedge: 308 Calories; 10.0 g Total Fat (1.5 g Mono, 0.5 g Poly, 4.5 g Sat); 25 mg Cholesterol; 41 g Carbohydrate; 7 g Fibre; 13 g Protein; 610 mg Sodium

Vegetarian

Spinach Potato Bake

This rich, cheesy casserole has lots of flavourful spinach and vegetables. It's a quiche-like dish that also makes a great brunch option.

Cooking oil	2 tsp.	10 mL
Diced peeled potato	4 cups	1 L
Chopped fennel bulb (white part only)	1 cup	250 mL
Chopped onion	1 cup	250 mL
Sliced celery	1 cup	250 mL
Garlic cloves, minced	2	2
(or 1/2 tsp., 2 mL, powder)		
Chopped fresh spinach leaves, lightly packed	6 cups	1.5 L
Large eggs	3	3
Ricotta cheese	2 cups	500 mL
Salt	1/2 tsp.	2 mL
Pepper	1/2 tsp.	2 mL
Grated Asiago cheese	1 cup	250 mL

Heat cooking oil in large frying pan on medium. Add next 5 ingredients. Cook for about 10 minutes, stirring often, until celery is softened.

Add spinach. Heat and stir for about 2 minutes until spinach is wilted. Remove from heat.

Whisk next 4 ingredients in large bowl.

Add Asiago cheese and spinach mixture. Stir. Transfer to greased 9 x 13 inch (23 x 33 cm) baking dish. Bake in 350°F (175°C) oven for about 50 minutes until knife inserted in centre comes out clean. Let stand for 10 minutes. Cuts into 8 pieces.

1 piece: 254 Calories; 14.0 g Total Fat (3.5 g Mono, 1.0 g Poly, 8.0 g Sat); 90 mg Cholesterol; 19 g Carbohydrate; 2 g Fibre; 14 g Protein; 379 mg Sodium

 tip If a recipe calls for less than an entire can of tomato paste, freeze the unopened can for 30 minutes. Open both ends and push the contents through one end. Slice off only what you need. Freeze the remaining paste in a resealable freezer bag or plastic wrap for future use.

Chickpea Pasta Casserole

An appetizing dish with hearty chickpeas, tangy tomatoes and creamy goat cheese. Any bite-sized pasta may be used in place of ditali, but refer to the package directions for varied cook times.

Water	8 cups	2 L
Salt	1 tsp.	5 mL
Ditali pasta	1 1/2 cups	375 mL
Chopped cauliflower	2 cups	500 mL
Can of diced tomatoes (with juice)	28 oz.	796 mL
Can of chickpeas (garbanzo beans), rinsed and drained	19 oz.	540 mL
Chopped zucchini (with peel)	1 cup	250 mL
Finely chopped onion	1/2 cup	125 mL
Goat (chèvre) cheese, cut up	4 oz.	113 g
Sun-dried tomato pesto	2 tbsp.	30 mL
Red wine vinegar	1 tbsp.	15 mL
Garlic cloves, minced (or 1/2 tsp., 2 mL, powder)	2	2
Granulated sugar	1/2 tsp.	2 mL
Crushed unseasoned croutons	1/2 cup	125 mL
Butter (or hard margarine), melted	1 tbsp.	15 mL

Combine water and salt in Dutch oven. Bring to a boil. Add pasta. Boil, uncovered, for 5 minutes, stirring occasionally.

Add cauliflower. Boil, uncovered, for about 2 minutes until pasta is tender but firm. Drain. Return to same pot.

Add next 9 ingredients. Stir well. Transfer to greased 9 x 13 inch (23 x 33 cm) baking dish.

Combine croutons and butter in small bowl. Sprinkle over pasta mixture. Bake in 350°F (175°C) oven for about 50 minutes until vegetables are tender. Serves 8.

1 serving: 236 Calories; 7.0 g Total Fat (1.5 g Mono, 1.0 g Poly, 2.5 g Sat); 8 mg Cholesterol; 35 g Carbohydrate; 5 g Fibre; 11 g Protein; 570 mg Sodium

Smoky Mac 'n' Cheese

This one's for all the fans of smoked cheese! This aromatic version of macaroni and cheese is comfort food at its finest.

Water	8 cups	2 L
Salt	1 tsp.	5 mL
Elbow macaroni	2 cups	500 mL
Butter (or hard margarine)	2 tbsp.	30 mL
Finely chopped onion	1/4 cup	60 mL
All-purpose flour	2 tbsp.	30 mL
Milk	2 cups	500 mL
Grated smoked Gouda cheese	1 cup	250 mL
Grated sharp Cheddar cheese	1/2 cup	125 mL
Grated Parmesan cheese	1/4 cup	60 mL
Dijon mustard	2 tsp.	10 mL
Salt	1/2 tsp.	2 mL
Cayenne pepper, just a pinch (optional)		
Fine dry bread crumbs	3 tbsp.	50 mL
Butter (or hard margarine), melted	1 tbsp.	15 mL

Combine water and salt in large saucepan. Bring to a boil. Add pasta. Boil, uncovered, for 8 to 10 minutes, stirring occasionally, until tender but firm. Drain. Transfer to greased 2 quart (2 L) casserole.

Melt butter in medium saucepan on medium. Add onion. Cook for about 3 minutes, stirring often, until softened.

Add flour. Heat and stir for 1 minute. Slowly add milk, stirring constantly until smooth. Heat and stir until boiling and thickened. Remove from heat.

Add next 6 ingredients. Stir until cheese is melted. Add to pasta. Stir until coated.

Combine bread crumbs and melted butter in small bowl. Sprinkle over pasta mixture. Bake, uncovered, in 350°F (175°C) oven for about 30 minutes until bubbling and golden. Serves 4.

1 serving: 585 Calories; 27.0 g Total Fat (5.0 g Mono, 0.5 g Poly, 16.0 g Sat); 87 mg Cholesterol; 57 g Carbohydrate; 2 g Fibre; 28 g Protein; 992 mg Sodium

Pictured on page 108.

Vegetarian

Rice Lentil Casserole

This convenient one-dish meal of lentils, rice, fresh-tasting tomatoes and mozzarella has deliciously satisfying flavour and texture.

Prepared vegetable broth	2 1/2 cups	625 mL
Can of diced tomatoes (with juice)	14 oz.	398 mL
Chopped onion	1 cup	250 mL
Diced carrot	1 cup	250 mL
Dried green lentils	3/4 cup	175 mL
Grated mozzarella cheese	3/4 cup	175 mL
Long-grain brown rice	3/4 cup	175 mL
Can of diced green chilies	4 oz.	113 g
Dried basil	1/2 tsp.	2 mL
Dried oregano	1/2 tsp.	2 mL
Garlic cloves, minced	2	2
(or 1/2 tsp., 2 mL, powder)		
Salt	1/4 tsp.	1 mL

Combine all 12 ingredients in greased 3 quart (3 L) casserole. Bake, covered, in 350°F (175°C) oven for about 90 minutes until lentils and rice are tender and liquid is absorbed. Makes about 6 cups (1.5 L).

1 cup (250 mL): 245 Calories; 4.0 g Total Fat (0 g Mono, 0 g Poly, 2.0 g Sat); 8 mg Cholesterol; 41 g Carbohydrate; 5 g Fibre; 13 g Protein; 869 mg Sodium

Eggplant Parmigiana Lasagna

This delicious vegetarian lasagna has rich and tangy flavours, with lots of eggplant and cheese. Leftover portions can be frozen and reheated.

Medium eggplant (with peel), about	1	1
1 1/4 lbs. (560 g)		
Salt, sprinkle		
Cooking oil	2 tsp.	10 mL
Chopped onion	1 cup	250 mL
Garlic cloves, minced	2	2
(or 1/2 tsp., 2 mL, powder)		

(continued on next page)

114   Vegetarian

Cans of tomato sauce (14 oz., 398 mL, each)	2	2
Can of diced tomatoes (with juice)	14 oz.	398 mL
Chopped fresh basil (or 3/4 tsp., 4 mL, dried)	1 tbsp.	15 mL
Oven-ready lasagna noodles	9	9
Grated Italian cheese blend	2 cups	500 mL

Cut eggplant crosswise into 1/4 inch (6 mm) slices. Discard outside slices. Sprinkle both sides of eggplant slices with salt. Transfer to large plate. Let stand for 1 hour. Rinse. Blot dry.

Heat cooking oil in large frying pan on medium. Add onion and garlic. Cook for about 5 minutes, stirring often, until onion is softened.

Add next 3 ingredients. Stir. Remove from heat.

To assemble, layer ingredients in greased 9 x 13 inch (23 x 33 cm) baking dish as follows:

1. 1/3 of tomato mixture
2. 3 lasagna noodles
3. Half of eggplant slices
4. 1/2 cup (125 mL) cheese
5. 1/3 of tomato mixture
6. 3 lasagna noodles
7. Remaining eggplant slices
8. 1/2 cup (125 mL) cheese
9. 3 lasagna noodles
10. Remaining tomato mixture
11. Remaining cheese

Cover with greased foil. Bake in 350°F (175°C) oven for about 90 minutes until eggplant and pasta are tender. Let stand, covered, for 10 minutes. Cuts into 8 pieces.

1 piece: 285 Calories; 8.0 g Total Fat (0.5 g Mono, 0 g Poly, 3.5 g Sat); 20 mg Cholesterol; 40 g Carbohydrate; 5 g Fibre; 14 g Protein; 960 mg Sodium

Pictured on page 54.

Paré Pointer
The bird that landed in a volcano cooked its own goose.

Vegetarian

Chipotle Bean Cannelloni

This all-in-one dish features black bean-filled cannelloni covered in tomato sauce and cheese. A smoky, spicy delight!

Cooking oil	1 tsp.	5 mL
Chopped onion	1 cup	250 mL
Finely chopped chipotle peppers in adobo sauce (see Tip, page 50)	2 tsp.	10 mL
Ground cumin	1 tsp.	5 mL
Garlic cloves, minced (or 1/2 tsp., 2 mL, powder)	2	2
Salt	1 tsp.	5 mL
Pepper	1/2 tsp.	2 mL
Fresh spinach leaves, lightly packed	6 cups	1.5 L
Can of black beans, rinsed and drained	19 oz.	540 mL
Red wine vinegar	2 tbsp.	30 mL
Chopped fresh cilantro (or parsley)	1 tbsp.	15 mL
Dry curd cottage cheese	1 cup	250 mL
Tomato pasta sauce	3 cups	750 mL
Water	1 1/2 cups	375 mL
Oven-ready cannelloni shells	18	18
Grated sharp Cheddar cheese	1 cup	250 mL

Heat cooking oil in large frying pan on medium. Add next 6 ingredients. Cook for about 5 minutes, stirring often, until onion is softened.

Add spinach. Heat and stir for about 2 minutes until spinach starts to wilt. Transfer to food processor.

Add next 3 ingredients. Process with on/off motion until smooth. Add cottage cheese. Process until combined.

Combine pasta sauce and water in medium bowl. Spread half of sauce mixture in greased 9 x 13 inch (23 x 33 cm) baking dish.

Spoon black bean mixture into large resealable freezer bag with piece snipped off corner. Pipe into pasta shells. Arrange in single layer over sauce mixture in baking dish. Pour remaining sauce mixture over top.

(continued on next page)

116   Vegetarian

Sprinkle with Cheddar cheese. Cover with greased foil. Bake in 350°F (175°C) oven for 45 minutes. Carefully remove foil. Bake for about 15 minutes until pasta is tender and cheese is melted. Let stand for 10 minutes. Makes 18 cannelloni.

1 cannelloni: 111 Calories; 4.0 g Total Fat (0 g Mono, 0 g Poly, 2.0 g Sat); 5 mg Cholesterol; 13 g Carbohydrate; 3 g Fibre; 9 g Protein; 494 mg Sodium

---

Pizza Pot Pie

Pizza is a perennial favourite, and this upside-down twist will have the kids running to the table—they might even be willing to help you prepare it! A thick, cheesy crust tops saucy veggie "toppings."

Cooking oil	2 tsp.	10 mL
Sliced fresh white mushrooms	4 cups	1 L
Chopped onion	1 cup	250 mL
Finely chopped celery	1/2 cup	125 mL
Tomato paste (see Tip, page 111)	2 tbsp.	30 mL
Chopped yellow pepper	2 cups	500 mL
Can of tomato sauce	7 1/2 oz.	213 mL
Dried oregano	1 tsp.	5 mL
Pepper	1/4 tsp.	1 mL
Tube of refrigerator pizza dough	14 oz.	391 g
Grated Italian cheese blend	3/4 cup	175 mL

Heat cooking oil in large frying pan on medium-high. Add next 3 ingredients. Cook for about 5 minutes, stirring often, until onion starts to soften.

Add tomato paste. Cook for about 5 minutes, stirring often, until liquid is almost evaporated. Remove from heat.

Add next 4 ingredients. Stir. Transfer to greased shallow 2 quart (2 L) casserole.

Roll out dough to fit casserole. Place over vegetable mixture.

Sprinkle with cheese. Bake, uncovered, in 375°F (190°C) oven for about 30 minutes until filling is bubbling at edges and top is golden brown. Serves 6.

1 serving: 274 Calories; 7.0 g Total Fat (1.0 g Mono, 0.5 g Poly, 2.5 g Sat); 10 mg Cholesterol; 43 g Carbohydrate; 3 g Fibre; 11 g Protein; 809 mg Sodium

Vegetarian

Quinoa Chimichurri Casserole

A colourful casserole of nutritious quinoa and potatoes, complete with lots of fresh herbs and a pleasant chili heat that builds.

Cooking oil	1 tsp.	5 mL
Chopped carrot	1 cup	250 mL
Chopped onion	1 cup	250 mL
Chopped peeled potato	3 cups	750 mL
Prepared vegetable broth	2 cups	500 mL
Fresh (or frozen, thawed) kernel corn	1 cup	250 mL
Quinoa, rinsed and drained	1 cup	250 mL
Dried crushed chilies	1/4 tsp.	1 mL
Coarsely chopped fresh cilantro	1/4 cup	60 mL
Coarsely chopped fresh parsley	1/4 cup	60 mL
Coarsely chopped fresh oregano	2 tbsp.	30 mL
Cooking oil	2 tbsp.	30 mL
Red wine vinegar	2 tbsp.	30 mL
Granulated sugar	1 tbsp.	15 mL
Garlic clove, minced	1	1
(or 1/4 tsp., 1 mL, powder)		
Salt	1/4 tsp.	1 mL
Pepper	1/8 tsp.	0.5 mL
Finely chopped red pepper	1 cup	250 mL

Heat cooking oil in medium frying pan on medium. Add carrot and onion. Cook for about 10 minutes, stirring often, until onion is softened. Transfer to greased 3 quart (3 L) casserole.

Add next 5 ingredients. Stir. Bake, covered, in 375°F (190°C) oven for about 75 minutes until vegetables and quinoa are tender.

Process next 9 ingredients in blender until smooth. Drizzle over potato mixture.

Add red pepper. Stir. Makes about 10 cups (2.5 L).

1 cup (250 mL): 174 Calories; 4.5 g Total Fat (2.5 g Mono, 1.5 g Poly, 0 g Sat); 0 mg Cholesterol; 30 g Carbohydrate; 4 g Fibre; 5 g Protein; 274 mg Sodium

Vegetarian

Veggie Taco Quiche

Tacos in a pan! All of your favourite taco ingredients packed into a quiche base, and topped with nacho chips—the kids will love it.

Yellow cornmeal	1 tbsp.	15 mL
Cooking oil	2 tsp.	10 mL
Chopped fresh white mushrooms	1 cup	250 mL
Chopped onion	1 cup	250 mL
Chopped red pepper	1 cup	250 mL
Chopped zucchini (with peel)	1 cup	250 mL
Fresh (or frozen, thawed) kernel corn	1/2 cup	125 mL
Chili powder	2 tsp.	10 mL
Dried oregano	1/2 tsp.	2 mL
Ground cumin	1/2 tsp.	2 mL
Salt	1/2 tsp.	2 mL
Pepper	1/4 tsp.	1 mL
Large eggs	8	8
Biscuit mix	1/2 cup	125 mL
Milk	1/2 cup	125 mL
Mild salsa	1/2 cup	125 mL
Sour cream	1/2 cup	125 mL
Grated Mexican cheese blend	1 cup	250 mL
Shredded iceberg lettuce, lightly packed	1 cup	250 mL
Crushed nacho chips	1/2 cup	125 mL

Sprinkle cornmeal into greased 9 x 13 inch (23 x 33 cm) baking dish.

Heat cooking oil in large frying pan on medium. Add next 10 ingredients. Cook for about 12 minutes, stirring often, until onion is softened. Spread evenly in prepared baking dish.

Beat next 3 ingredients until smooth. Pour over vegetable mixture. Bake in 350°F (175°C) oven for about 30 minutes until knife inserted in centre of quiche comes out clean. Let stand in pan on wire rack for 10 minutes.

Combine salsa and sour cream in small bowl. Spread over quiche.

Scatter remaining 3 ingredients over top. Cuts into 8 pieces.

1 piece: 240 Calories; 14.0 g Total Fat (2.5 g Mono, 1.0 g Poly, 6.0 g Sat); 156 mg Cholesterol; 19 g Carbohydrate; 2 g Fibre; 11 g Protein; 540 mg Sodium

Vegetarian

Ruffled Spinach Bean Bake

Attractive phyllo tops a hearty and delicious filling of beans, spinach, feta and tomato.

Cooking oil	2 tsp.	10 mL
Chopped onion	1 cup	250 mL
Chopped celery	1/2 cup	125 mL
Finely chopped carrot	1/2 cup	125 mL
Garlic cloves, minced	2	2
(or 1/2 tsp., 2 mL, powder)		
Can of mixed beans, rinsed and drained	19 oz.	540 mL
Chopped fresh spinach leaves,	2 cups	500 mL
lightly packed		
Chopped tomato	1 cup	250 mL
Can of tomato sauce	7 1/2 oz.	213 mL
Brown sugar, packed	1 tbsp.	15 mL
Dried oregano	1 tsp.	5 mL
Paprika	1 tsp.	5 mL
Dry mustard	1/2 tsp.	2 mL
Salt	1/4 tsp.	1 mL
Pepper	1/4 tsp.	1 mL
Crumbled feta cheese	1/4 cup	60 mL
Phyllo pastry sheets, thawed according	4	4
to package directions		
Butter (or hard margarine), melted	2 tbsp.	30 mL

Heat cooking oil in large frying pan on medium. Add next 3 ingredients. Cook for about 10 minutes, stirring often, until celery is softened.

Add garlic. Heat and stir for about 1 minute until fragrant.

Add next 10 ingredients. Cook for about 5 minutes, stirring occasionally, until heated through. Transfer to greased 2 quart (2 L) casserole.

Sprinkle with cheese.

(continued on next page)

Vegetarian

Place 1 pastry sheet on work surface. Cover remaining sheets with damp towel to prevent drying. Brush sheet with butter. Bunch up loosely. Place over cheese. Repeat with remaining pastry sheets and butter. Bake, uncovered, in 375°F (190°C) oven for about 20 minutes until pastry is golden. Serves 4.

1 serving: 327 Calories; 12.0 g Total Fat (4.0 g Mono, 1.5 g Poly, 6.0 g Sat); 24 mg Cholesterol; 46 g Carbohydrate; 8 g Fibre; 12 g Protein; 785 mg Sodium

Pictured on page 125.

Curry Orzo Casserole

A colourful risotto-like pasta casserole with warm curry spices and a pleasant texture from mushrooms and veggies.

Cooking oil	2 tsp.	10 mL
Chopped fresh white mushrooms	3 cups	750 mL
Chopped onion	1 cup	250 mL
Garlic cloves, minced	2	2
(or 1/2 tsp., 2 mL, powder)		
Mild curry paste	2 tbsp.	30 mL
Granulated sugar	1/2 tsp.	2 mL
Salt	1/4 tsp.	1 mL
Pepper	1/4 tsp.	1 mL
Prepared vegetable broth	3 cups	750 mL
Chopped red pepper	2 cups	500 mL
Frozen peas	2 cups	500 mL
Orzo	2 cups	500 mL

Heat cooking oil in large frying pan on medium. Add next 3 ingredients. Cook for about 10 minutes, stirring often, until onion is softened.

Add next 4 ingredients. Heat and stir for 1 minute. Transfer to greased 9 x 13 inch (23 x 33 cm) baking dish.

Add remaining 4 ingredients. Stir. Bake, covered, in 400°F (205°C) oven for about 35 minutes, stirring at halftime, until pasta is tender. Stir. Let stand, covered, for 10 minutes. Makes about 8 cups (2 L).

1 cup (250 mL): 140 Calories; 2.0 g Total Fat (0.5 g Mono, 0.5 g Poly, 0 g Sat); 0 mg Cholesterol; 24 g Carbohydrate; 3 g Fibre; 6 g Protein; 598 mg Sodium

Bean-Stuffed Portobellos

Intriguing flavours make for a sophisticated vegetarian main course—mushroom caps stuffed with bold goat cheese, beans and red pepper.

Small portobello mushrooms, stems and gills removed (see Note)	4	4
Cooking oil	2 tsp.	10 mL
Canned white kidney beans, rinsed and drained	1 cup	250 mL
Chopped arugula, lightly packed	1 cup	250 mL
Finely chopped red pepper	1/4 cup	60 mL
Balsamic vinegar	1 tbsp.	15 mL
Cooking oil	1 tbsp.	15 mL
Chopped fresh rosemary (or 1/4 tsp., 1 mL, dried, crushed)	1 tsp.	5 mL
Garlic clove, minced (or 1/4 tsp., 1 mL, powder)	1	1
Salt	1/4 tsp.	1 mL
Pepper	1/4 tsp.	1 mL
Goat (chèvre) cheese, cut up	4 oz.	113 g

Brush mushrooms with first amount of cooking oil. Arrange, stem-side up, in 9 x 9 inch (23 x 23 cm) pan.

Combine next 9 ingredients in small bowl. Spoon into mushroom caps.

Scatter cheese over top. Cover with greased foil. Bake in 375°F (190°C) oven for 10 minutes. Carefully remove foil. Bake for about 5 minutes until mushrooms are tender and cheese is melted. Makes 4 stuffed portobellos.

1 stuffed portobello: 179 Calories; 10.0 g Total Fat (4.5 g Mono, 2.0 g Poly, 3.0 g Sat); 9 mg Cholesterol; 15 g Carbohydrate; 5 g Fibre; 9 g Protein; 383 mg Sodium

Pictured on page 125.

Note: Because the gills can sometimes be bitter, be sure to remove them from the portobellos before stuffing. First remove the stems. Then, using a small spoon, scrape out and discard the gills.

Baked "Fried" Rice

Favourite fried rice flavours prepared in the oven! This colourful casserole has browned tofu and veggies with appealing soy and chili flavours. If you have sesame oil on hand, you can add a teaspoon before serving to punch up the sesame flavour even more.

Long-grain white rice	2 cups	500 mL
Prepared vegetable broth	2 cups	500 mL
Chopped fresh white mushrooms	1 cup	250 mL
Finely chopped onion	1 cup	250 mL
Water	1 cup	250 mL
Soy sauce	2 tbsp.	30 mL
Salt	1/8 tsp.	0.5 mL
Pepper	1/4 tsp.	1 mL
Package of firm tofu, cut into 1/2 inch (12 mm) pieces	12 1/4 oz.	350 g
Chili paste (sambal oelek)	1 tsp.	5 mL
Soy sauce	1 tsp.	5 mL
Sesame (or cooking) oil	2 tsp.	10 mL
Frozen pea and carrot mix, thawed	1 cup	250 mL
Broccoli slaw	1/2 cup	125 mL
Finely chopped orange pepper	1/2 cup	125 mL

Combine first 8 ingredients in 9 x 13 inch (23 x 33 cm) baking dish. Bake, covered, in 375°F (190°C) oven for about 45 minutes until rice is almost tender.

Toss next 3 ingredients in small bowl until tofu is coated. Heat sesame oil in large frying pan on medium-high. Add tofu. Cook for about 6 minutes, stirring often, until browned.

Add remaining 3 ingredients and tofu to rice mixture. Stir. Bake, covered, for about 10 minutes until rice and vegetables are tender. Let stand, covered, for about 10 minutes until liquid is absorbed. Makes about 8 1/2 cups (2.1 L).

1 cup (250 mL): 229 Calories; 3.0 g Total Fat (0.5 g Mono, 1.0 g Poly, 0.5 g Sat); 0 mg Cholesterol; 42 g Carbohydrate; 1 g Fibre; 9 g Protein; 436 mg Sodium

Pictured on page 125.

Vegetarian

Seasoned Vegetable Quinoa

A cheery-looking quinoa casserole with roasted sweet potato and red pepper—nicely seasoned and pleasantly filling.

Cubed peeled orange-fleshed sweet potato (3/4 inch, 2 cm, pieces)	3 cups	750 mL
Chopped red pepper (1 inch, 2.5 cm, pieces)	1 1/2 cups	375 mL
Chopped onion (1 inch, 2.5 cm, pieces)	1 cup	250 mL
Cooking oil	2 tbsp.	30 mL
Greek seasoning	1 tbsp.	15 mL
Coarsely ground pepper	3/4 tsp.	4 mL
Garlic cloves, minced (or 1/4 tsp., 1 mL, powder)	1	1
Boiling water	1 cup	250 mL
Quinoa, rinsed and drained	1 cup	250 mL
Vegetable cocktail juice	1 cup	250 mL

Toss first 7 ingredients in large bowl. Spread in ungreased 9 x 13 inch (23 x 33 cm) pan. Bake in 425°F (220°C) oven for 30 minutes.

Carefully add boiling water.

Add quinoa and vegetable cocktail juice. Stir. Bake, covered, for about 20 minutes until quinoa is tender and liquid is absorbed. Makes about 6 cups (1.5 L).

1 cup (250 mL): 231 Calories; 6.0 g Total Fat (3.0 g Mono, 2.0 g Poly, 0.5 g Sat); 0 mg Cholesterol; 39 g Carbohydrate; 5 g Fibre; 6 g Protein; 154 mg Sodium

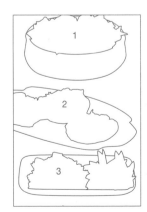

1. Ruffled Spinach Bean Bake, page 120
2. Bean-Stuffed Portobellos, page 122
3. Baked "Fried" Rice, page 123

Vegetarian

Herbed Corn Cob Bake

An entirely unexpected method for cooking corn on the cob! This easy-to-make side dish boasts fresh herb flavour.

Butter (or hard margarine), melted	3 tbsp.	50 mL
Chopped fresh chives (or green onion)	2 tsp.	10 mL
Chopped fresh parsley (or 1/2 tsp., 2 mL, flakes)	2 tsp.	10 mL
Chopped fresh thyme (or 1/4 tsp., 1 mL, dried)	1 tsp.	5 mL
Lemon juice	1 tsp.	5 mL
Paprika	1/4 tsp.	1 mL
Salt	1/8 tsp.	0.5 mL
Coarsely ground pepper	1/8 tsp.	0.5 mL
Medium corncobs, cut crosswise into 2 inch (5 cm) pieces	4	4
Grated Parmesan cheese	2 tbsp.	30 mL

Combine first 8 ingredients in small cup.

Arrange corn in shallow 2 quart (2 L) casserole. Brush with butter mixture. Bake, covered, in 375°F (190°C) oven for about 30 minutes until corn is tender.

Sprinkle with cheese. Serves 6.

1 serving: 103 Calories; 7.0 g Total Fat (2.0 g Mono, 0.5 g Poly, 4.0 g Sat); 17 mg Cholesterol; 10 g Carbohydrate; 1 g Fibre; 2 g Protein; 120 mg Sodium

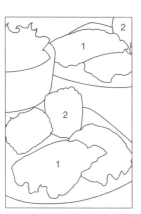

Pictured at left.

1. Slow-Roasted Ribs, page 88
2. Herbed Corn Cob Bake, above

Yorkshire Pudding

This golden Yorkshire pudding makes a great casual side for serving with a roast beef dinner—deliciously traditional flavours.

All-purpose flour	1 cup	250 mL
Salt	1/2 tsp.	2 mL
Pepper	1/4 tsp.	1 mL
Large eggs	3	3
Milk	1 cup	250 mL
Grated onion	1 tbsp.	15 mL
Cooking oil	2 tbsp.	30 mL

Combine first 3 ingredients in medium bowl. Make a well in centre.

Whisk next 3 ingredients in small bowl. Add to well. Whisk until smooth. Let stand, covered, for 30 minutes.

Pour cooking oil into 9 x 13 inch (23 x 33 cm) pan. Heat in 400°F (205°C) oven for about 5 minutes until oil is hot. Remove from oven. Brush oil over bottom of pan. Stir batter. Carefully pour into prepared pan. Bake for about 25 minutes until puffed and golden. Cuts into 12 pieces.

1 piece: 82 Calories; 3.5 g Total Fat (1.5 g Mono, 1.0 g Poly, 0.5 g Sat); 35 mg Cholesterol; 9 g Carbohydrate; trace Fibre; 3 g Protein; 104 mg Sodium

Greek Potato Bake

Lemon and garlic flavours permeate golden potatoes topped with a lovely parsley sprinkle. Simple and delicious!

Olive (or cooking) oil	2 tbsp.	30 mL
Dried oregano	1 tsp.	5 mL
Garlic cloves, minced	2	2
(or 1/2 tsp., 2 mL, powder)		
Salt	1/4 tsp.	1 mL
Coarsely ground pepper	1/4 tsp.	1 mL
Red baby potatoes, larger ones halved	2 lbs.	900 g
Lemon juice	1/4 cup	60 mL
Prepared chicken broth	1/4 cup	60 mL
Chopped fresh parsley	1 tbsp.	15 mL

(continued on next page)

128 Sides

Combine first 5 ingredients in large bowl. Add potatoes. Toss until coated. Transfer to greased 9 x 13 inch (23 x 33 cm) baking dish.

Combine lemon juice and broth in small bowl. Drizzle over potatoes. Bake in 400°F (205°C) oven for about 40 minutes, stirring at halftime, until potatoes are golden and tender.

Sprinkle with parsley. Makes about 7 cups (1.75 L).

1 cup (250 mL): 146 Calories; 4.0 g Total Fat (2.5 g Mono, 1.0 g Poly, 0 g Sat); 0 mg Cholesterol; 24 g Carbohydrate; 2 g Fibre; 3 g Protein; 86 mg Sodium

Spring Veggie Cornbread

This moist cornbread with rows of fresh asparagus is full of herb flavour. Serve right from the pan to accompany salmon or roast. Reheat leftover pieces in the microwave for just-baked freshness.

All-purpose flour	1 1/2 cups	375 mL
Yellow cornmeal	1 cup	250 mL
Baking powder	2 tsp.	10 mL
Dried dillweed	2 tsp.	10 mL
Dried basil	1 tsp.	5 mL
Baking soda	1/2 tsp.	2 mL
Salt	1/2 tsp.	2 mL
Pepper	1/4 tsp.	1 mL
Large eggs	2	2
Buttermilk (or soured milk, see Tip, page 94)	1 1/2 cups	375 mL
Cooking oil	1/3 cup	75 mL
Sliced green onion	1/4 cup	60 mL
Fresh asparagus tips (3 inch, 7.5 cm, length)	12	12

Combine first 8 ingredients in medium bowl. Make a well in centre.

Whisk next 4 ingredients in small bowl. Add to well. Stir until just moistened. Spread in greased 9 x 9 inch (23 x 23 cm) pan.

Arrange asparagus over top. Bake in 350°F (175°C) oven for about 25 minutes until wooden pick inserted in centre comes out clean. Let stand in pan on wire rack for 10 minutes. Cuts into 9 squares.

1 square: 250 Calories; 9.0 g Total Fat (4.5 g Mono, 2.5 g Poly, 1.0 g Sat); 33 mg Cholesterol; 34 g Carbohydrate; 1 g Fibre; 6 g Protein; 252 mg Sodium

Italian Sausage Stuffing

This homemade stuffing has the rich flavours and appetizing textures of soft bread, crunchy hazelnuts and spicy sausage.

Hot Italian sausage, casing removed	1/2 lb.	225 g
Chopped fresh white mushrooms	4 cups	1 L
Chopped celery	2 cups	500 mL
Chopped onion	2 cups	500 mL
Fennel seed, crushed (see Tip, below)	1 tsp.	5 mL
Garlic cloves, minced	2	2
(or 1/2 tsp., 2 mL, powder)		
Salt	1/2 tsp.	2 mL
Pepper	1/4 tsp.	1 mL
Whole-wheat bread cubes	8 cups	2 L
Large eggs, fork-beaten	2	2
Prepared chicken broth	1 cup	250 mL
Chopped flaked hazelnuts (filberts), toasted (see Tip, page 86)	1/4 cup	60 mL
Butter (or hard margarine), melted	2 tbsp.	30 mL
Dried sage	1/4 tsp.	1 mL

Scramble-fry sausage in large frying pan on medium-high for about 5 minutes until browned. Transfer to paper towel-lined plate to drain. Drain and discard all but 1 tsp. (5 mL) drippings. Reduce heat to medium.

Add next 7 ingredients. Cook for about 10 minutes, stirring often, until liquid is almost evaporated. Transfer to large bowl.

Add bread cubes and sausage. Stir.

Combine remaining 5 ingredients in small bowl. Pour over bread mixture. Stir well. Transfer to greased 3 quart (3 L) casserole. Bake, covered, in 375°F (190°C) oven for 15 minutes. Remove cover. Bake for about 25 minutes until top is golden. Makes about 10 cups (2.5 L).

1 cup (250 mL): 245 Calories; 13.0 g Total Fat (6.0 g Mono, 1.5 g Poly, 4.5 g Sat); 45 mg Cholesterol; 23 g Carbohydrate; 4 g Fibre; 11 g Protein; 636 mg Sodium

 tip To crush fennel seed, place in large resealable freezer bag. Seal bag. Gently hit with flat side of meat mallet or with rolling pin.

Cheesy Broccoli Bake

A rich and cheesy broccoli dish, perfectly portioned for weeknights at home.
This recipe doubles easily to serve a crowd or take to a potluck—just be sure to
use a 2 quart (2 L) casserole dish.

Broccoli florets	3 cups	750 mL
Ice water		
Herb and garlic cream cheese	1/2 cup	125 mL
Milk	1/4 cup	60 mL
Salt, sprinkle		
Pepper, sprinkle		
Large hard-cooked egg (see Note), finely chopped	1	1
Whole-wheat (or white) bread slices, processed into crumbs	2	2
Butter (or hard margarine), melted	1 tbsp.	15 mL
Chopped fresh parsley (or 1/2 tsp., 2 mL, flakes)	1 tbsp.	15 mL

Pour water into medium saucepan until about 1 inch (2.5 cm) deep. Bring to a boil. Reduce heat to medium. Add broccoli. Boil gently, covered, for about 2 minutes until bright green. Drain. Plunge broccoli into ice water in large bowl. Let stand for about 10 minutes until cold. Drain.

Combine next 4 ingredients in same pot. Heat and stir on medium until smooth. Remove from heat. Add broccoli. Stir until coated. Transfer to greased 1 quart (1 L) casserole.

Combine remaining 4 ingredients in small bowl. Scatter over broccoli mixture. Bake, uncovered, in 375°F (190°C) oven for about 20 minutes until topping is golden and broccoli is heated through. Serves 4.

1 serving: 164 Calories; 11.0 g Total Fat (1.5 g Mono, 0 g Poly, 6.0 g Sat); 63 mg Cholesterol; 13 g Carbohydrate; 3 g Fibre; 6 g Protein; 239 mg Sodium

Note: To make hard-cooked eggs, place eggs in a single layer in a saucepan. Add cold water until it's about 1 inch (2.5 cm) above the eggs. Bring to a boil, covered. Reduce heat to medium-low. Simmer for 10 minutes. Drain. Cover the eggs with cold water. Change the water each time it warms until the eggs are cool enough to handle. Remove the shells.

Scalloped Potatoes

You can't go wrong when you serve this broadly appealing casserole classic, made in the old-fashioned way. These golden scalloped potatoes are topped with Asiago for a special flavour. This recipe should not be doubled, but it already makes a batch big enough for company.

Cooking oil	1 tsp.	5 mL
Sliced onion	2 cups	500 mL
Garlic cloves, minced	2	2
(or 1/2 tsp., 2 mL, powder)		
Salt	1/4 tsp.	1 mL
All-purpose flour	2 tbsp.	30 mL
Dried thyme	1/4 tsp.	1 mL
Salt	1/4 tsp.	1 mL
Pepper	1/4 tsp.	1 mL
Thinly sliced peeled baking potato (see Note)	6 cups	1.5 L
Milk	1 cup	250 mL
Prepared chicken (or vegetable) broth	1/2 cup	125 mL
Grated Asiago cheese	3/4 cup	175 mL

Heat cooking oil in large frying pan on medium. Add next 3 ingredients. Cook for about 10 minutes, stirring often, until onion is softened.

Combine next 4 ingredients in small cup.

To assemble, layer ingredients in greased 9 x 13 inch (23 x 33 cm) baking dish as follows:

1. 1/3 of potato slices
2. Half of flour mixture
3. Half of onion mixture
4. 1/3 of potato slices
5. Remaining flour mixture
6. Remaining onion mixture
7. Remaining potato slices

Combine milk and broth in small bowl. Pour over top. Cover with greased foil. Bake in 350°F (175°C) oven for 1 hour. Carefully remove foil.

(continued on next page)

Sprinkle with cheese. Bake for about 15 minutes until cheese is melted and golden. Serves 8.

1 serving: 149 Calories; 2.5 g Total Fat (0 g Mono, 0 g Poly, 1.0 g Sat); 6 mg Cholesterol; 26 g Carbohydrate; 2 g Fibre; 6 g Protein; 241 mg Sodium

Note: Evenly sliced potatoes are one of the secrets to a good scallop. Use a mandoline slicer or food processor to ensure equal thickness.

Double-Corn Pudding

Densely textured pudding with lots of sweet corn and a peppery finish—this makes a nice side for your festive ham or turkey. This recipe cannot be doubled.

Butter (or hard margarine)	3 tbsp.	50 mL
Frozen kernel corn	3/4 cup	175 mL
Finely chopped onion	1/2 cup	125 mL
Milk	2 cups	500 mL
Granulated sugar	1/2 tsp.	2 mL
Salt	3/4 tsp.	4 mL
Pepper	1/2 tsp.	2 mL
Yellow cornmeal	3/4 cup	175 mL
Milk	1/2 cup	125 mL
Large eggs, fork-beaten	2	2

Melt butter in large saucepan on medium. Add corn and onion. Cook for about 5 minutes, stirring often, until onion is softened.

Add next 4 ingredients. Heat and stir for about 5 minutes until hot, but not boiling.

Slowly add cornmeal, stirring constantly. Heat and stir until mixture is thickened. Remove from heat.

Stir in second amount of milk.

Add eggs. Stir well. Spread in greased 2 quart (2 L) casserole. Bake, uncovered, in 350°F (175°C) oven for about 45 minutes until puffed and golden. Let stand for 10 minutes. Serves 6.

1 serving: 213 Calories; 8.0 g Total Fat (2.0 g Mono, 0 g Poly, 4.5 g Sat); 65 mg Cholesterol; 27 g Carbohydrate; trace Fibre; 8 g Protein; 441 mg Sodium

Sides

Chow Mein Casserole

Experience your favourite take-out flavours, without leaving home! Tasty soy and ginger flavours come together in this fun side dish.

Fresh, thin Chinese-style egg noodles	4 oz.	113 g
Boiling water, to cover		
Broccoli florets	1 1/2 cups	375 mL
Chopped onion	1 cup	250 mL
Chopped red pepper	1 cup	250 mL
Sliced celery	1 cup	250 mL
Sliced fresh white mushrooms	1 cup	250 mL
Can of sliced water chestnuts, drained	8 oz.	227 mL
Prepared vegetable broth	1/2 cup	125 mL
Soy sauce	3 tbsp.	50 mL
Cornstarch	2 tsp.	10 mL
Finely grated ginger root	2 tsp.	10 mL
(or 1/2 tsp., 2 mL, ground ginger)		
Sesame oil (for flavour)	2 tsp.	10 mL
Garlic cloves, minced	2	2
(or 1/2 tsp., 2 mL, powder)		
Fresh bean sprouts	1/4 cup	60 mL
Roasted sesame seeds	2 tsp.	10 mL

Place noodles in large heatproof bowl. Pour boiling water over top. Let stand for about 5 minutes until tender. Drain. Cut several times with scissors.

Add next 6 ingredients. Stir.

Combine next 6 ingredients in small bowl. Pour over noodle mixture. Stir. Transfer to greased 3 quart (3 L) casserole. Bake, covered, in 350°F (175°C) oven for about 40 minutes until vegetables are tender-crisp and sauce is thickened. Stir.

Scatter bean sprouts and sesame seeds over top. Makes about 4 1/2 cups (1.1 L).

1 cup (250 mL): 120 Calories; 3.5 g Total Fat (0 g Mono, 0 g Poly, 0.5 g Sat); 4 mg Cholesterol; 18 g Carbohydrate; 4 g Fibre; 5 g Protein; 777 mg Sodium

Green Bean Mushroom Casserole

A golden crumb-topped green bean and mushroom casserole with creamy dill sauce—a classic side to pair with a variety of meals.

Butter (or hard margarine)	2 tbsp.	30 mL
Chopped onion	1 cup	250 mL
Sliced fresh white mushrooms	3 cups	750 mL
Garlic clove, minced	1	1
(or 1/4 tsp., 1 mL, powder)		
All-purpose flour	3 tbsp.	50 mL
Dried dillweed	3/4 tsp.	4 mL
Salt	1/4 tsp.	1 mL
Milk	1 cup	250 mL
Prepared vegetable broth	1/2 cup	125 mL
Frozen cut green beans, thawed	6 cups	1.5 L
Fine dry bread crumbs	1/2 cup	125 mL
Butter (or hard margarine), melted	1 tbsp.	15 mL
Pepper	1/4 tsp.	1 mL

Melt butter in large frying pan on medium. Add onion. Cook for about 5 minutes, stirring often, until softened.

Add mushrooms and garlic. Cook for about 10 minutes, stirring occasionally, until mushrooms are softened. Transfer 1/2 cup (125 mL) with slotted spoon to small bowl.

Add next 3 ingredients to remaining onion mixture. Heat and stir for 1 minute. Slowly add milk, stirring constantly until smooth. Add broth. Heat and stir until boiling and thickened.

Add beans. Stir. Transfer to greased shallow 2 quart (2 L) casserole.

Add remaining 3 ingredients to reserved onion mixture. Stir. Scatter over green bean mixture. Bake, uncovered, in 375°F (190°C) oven for about 30 minutes until topping is golden. Serves 8.

1 serving: 127 Calories; 5.0 g Total Fat (1.0 g Mono, 0 g Poly, 3.0 g Sat); 15 mg Cholesterol; 16 g Carbohydrate; 3 g Fibre; 5 g Protein; 235 mg Sodium

Dutch-Style Potato Bake

Tender, flavourful potatoes with bacon, sauerkraut and tart apple—this side is inspired by a Dutch dish in which similar ingredients are mashed together and eaten with sausage.

Chopped peeled potato	5 cups	1.25 L
Chopped peeled tart apple (such as Granny Smith)	2 cups	500 mL
Sauerkraut, rinsed and drained	1 1/2 cups	375 mL
Cooking oil	3 tbsp.	50 mL
Dijon mustard	2 tsp.	10 mL
Salt	1/2 tsp.	2 mL
Pepper	1/4 tsp.	1 mL
Bacon slices, cooked crisp and crumbled	3	3
Thinly sliced green onion	2 tbsp.	30 mL

Toss first 7 ingredients in large bowl. Transfer to greased 9 x 13 inch (23 x 33 cm) pan. Bake in 400°F (205°C) oven for about 1 hour, stirring occasionally, until potato and apple are tender and starting to brown.

Scatter bacon and green onion over top. Makes about 5 cups (1.25 L).

1 cup (250 mL): 250 Calories; 10.0 g Total Fat (6.0 g Mono, 2.5 g Poly, 1.5 g Sat); 5 mg Cholesterol; 35 g Carbohydrate; 5 g Fibre; 5 g Protein; 681 mg Sodium

Pictured on page 143.

Rice Pilaf

Simple to put together, this dressed-up rice can be served with dinner any night of the week.

Cooking oil	1 tsp.	5 mL
Diced carrot	1/4 cup	60 mL
Diced celery	1/4 cup	60 mL
Diced onion	1/4 cup	60 mL
Diced red pepper	1/4 cup	60 mL
Salt	1/4 tsp.	1 mL
Pepper	1/4 tsp.	1 mL

(continued on next page)

Converted white rice	1 1/2 cups	375 mL
Prepared chicken broth	3 cups	750 mL

Heat cooking oil in large saucepan on medium. Add next 6 ingredients. Cook for about 5 minutes, stirring often, until onion is softened.

Add rice. Heat and stir for about 1 minute until coated. Transfer to greased 2 quart (2 L) casserole.

Add broth. Stir. Bake, covered, in 375°F (190°C) oven for about 50 minutes until rice is tender and liquid is absorbed. Fluff with fork. Makes about 6 cups (1.5 L).

1 cup (250 mL): 188 Calories; 1.0 g Total Fat (0 g Mono, 0 g Poly, 0 g Sat); 0 mg Cholesterol; 40 g Carbohydrate; trace Fibre; 5 g Protein; 230 mg Sodium

---

Sweet-and-Sour Beans

You can't have a casual barbecue without baked beans making an appearance! The saucy sweetness and smoky barbecue flavour of these beans certainly fit the bill.

Cooking oil	1 tsp.	5 mL
Chopped onion	3/4 cup	175 mL
Can of romano beans, rinsed and drained	19 oz.	540 mL
Can of baked beans in tomato sauce	14 oz.	398 mL
Hickory barbecue sauce	1/3 cup	75 mL
Brown sugar, packed	2 tbsp.	30 mL
White vinegar	2 tbsp.	30 mL
Fancy (mild) molasses	1 tbsp.	15 mL
Prepared mustard	1 tsp.	5 mL

Heat cooking oil in small frying pan on medium. Add onion. Cook for about 5 minutes, stirring often, until softened. Transfer to ungreased 2 quart (2 L) casserole.

Add remaining 7 ingredients. Stir. Bake, covered, in 350°F (175°C) oven for about 1 hour until bubbling and heated through. Makes about 4 1/2 cups (1.1 L).

1 cup (250 mL): 225 Calories; 2.0 g Total Fat (0.5 g Mono, 0 g Poly, 0 g Sat); 0 mg Cholesterol; 49 g Carbohydrate; 6 g Fibre; 5 g Protein; 970 mg Sodium

Cheesy Bruschetta Zucchini

This side dish is certainly reminiscent of its appetizer namesake. Loaded with tomatoes, zucchini, croutons and a good dose of cheese, of course!

Diced zucchini (with peel)	3 cups	750 mL
Coarsely crushed unseasoned croutons (see Note)	1/3 cup	75 mL
Chopped seeded Roma (plum) tomato	2 cups	500 mL
Chopped green onion	1/4 cup	60 mL
Chopped fresh basil (or 1 1/2 tsp., 7 mL, dried)	2 tbsp.	30 mL
Cooking oil	1 tbsp.	15 mL
Balsamic vinegar	1 tsp.	5 mL
Garlic clove, minced (or 1/4 tsp., 1 mL, powder)	1	1
Salt	1/4 tsp.	1 mL
Grated Italian cheese blend	1 cup	250 mL
Coarsely crushed unseasoned croutons (see Note)	1/2 cup	125 mL

Combine zucchini and first amount of croutons in greased 8 x 8 inch (20 x 20 cm) baking dish.

Combine next 7 ingredients in medium bowl. Spoon over zucchini mixture. Bake in 375°F (190°C) oven for 20 minutes.

Combine cheese and second amount of croutons in small bowl. Scatter over tomato mixture. Bake for about 10 minutes until zucchini is tender-crisp and topping is golden. Serves 6.

1 serving: 120 Calories; 7.0 g Total Fat (1.5 g Mono, 1.0 g Poly, 2.5 g Sat); 13 mg Cholesterol; 8 g Carbohydrate; 2 g Fibre; 7 g Protein; 281 mg Sodium

Pictured on page 143.

Note: You can use coarse dry bread crumbs that look like croutons, or make your own by cutting bread into small cubes and drying in a low oven.

Paré Pointer

Don't tease egg whites—they can't take a yolk.

Apple Gingerbread Cobbler

Enjoy warm and comforting flavours—a cake-like gingerbread layer tops sweet-tart apples for a complementary combination.

Chopped peeled tart apple (such as Granny Smith)	5 cups	1.25 L
Lemon juice	2 tbsp.	30 mL
Brown sugar, packed	1/4 cup	60 mL
Butter (or hard margarine)	2 tbsp.	30 mL
All-purpose flour	1 tbsp.	15 mL
Ground cinnamon	1/4 tsp.	1 mL
All-purpose flour	1 1/4 cups	300 mL
Brown sugar, packed	1/4 cup	60 mL
Baking powder	1 tsp.	5 mL
Baking soda	1/4 tsp.	1 mL
Ground cinnamon	1/4 tsp.	1 mL
Ground cloves	1/4 tsp.	1 mL
Salt	1/4 tsp.	1 mL
Cold butter (or hard margarine), cut up	2 tbsp.	30 mL
Large egg	1	1
Milk	2/3 cup	150 mL
Fancy (mild) molasses	2 tbsp.	30 mL
Vanilla extract	1 tsp.	5 mL
Minced crystallized ginger	3 tbsp.	50 mL

Toss apple and lemon juice in large bowl until coated.

Add next 4 ingredients. Stir. Spread in 8 x 8 inch (20 x 20 cm) baking dish. Bake, covered, in 400°F (205°C) oven for 30 minutes.

Combine next 7 ingredients in medium bowl. Cut in second amount of butter until mixture resembles coarse crumbs. Make a well in centre.

Whisk next 4 ingredients in small bowl. Add to well.

Add ginger. Stir until just combined. Drop by mounded tablespoonfuls over hot apple mixture. Bake in 375°F (190°C) oven for about 30 minutes until apple is tender and wooden pick inserted in centre of biscuit comes out clean. Let stand on wire rack for 10 minutes. Serves 8.

1 serving: 268 Calories; 7.0 g Total Fat (1.5 g Mono, 0 g Poly, 4.0 g Sat); 33 mg Cholesterol; 49 g Carbohydrate; 2 g Fibre; 4 g Protein; 204 mg Sodium

Desserts

Chocolate Cookie Brownies

Rich, moist brownies top a layer of chocolate-coconut cookie for a unique mix of textures that makes for a satisfying treat.

Large egg	1	1
Butter (or hard margarine), softened	1/2 cup	125 mL
Granulated sugar	1/4 cup	60 mL
All-purpose flour	2/3 cup	150 mL
Cocoa, sifted if lumpy	1/3 cup	75 mL
Medium unsweetened coconut	1/3 cup	75 mL
Finely chopped pecans	1/4 cup	60 mL
All-purpose flour	3/4 cup	175 mL
Cocoa, sifted if lumpy	1/2 cup	125 mL
Salt	1/4 tsp.	1 mL
Large eggs	2	2
Granulated sugar	1 cup	250 mL
Semi-sweet chocolate chips	1 cup	250 mL
Butter (or hard margarine), melted	1/3 cup	75 mL

Beat first 3 ingredients in medium bowl until light and fluffy.

Add next 4 ingredients. Stir until no dry flour remains. Press into greased 9 x 9 inch (23 x 23 cm) pan.

Combine next 3 ingredients in large bowl. Make a well in centre.

Combine remaining 4 ingredients in small bowl. Add to well. Stir until just moistened. Spread over bottom layer. Bake in 350°F (175°C) oven for about 30 minutes until wooden pick inserted in centre of brownie comes out moist but not wet with batter. Do not overbake. Let stand in pan on wire rack until cool. Cuts into 36 squares.

1 square: 131 Calories; 7.0 g Total Fat (1.5 g Mono, 0 g Poly, 4.0 g Sat); 23 mg Cholesterol; 16 g Carbohydrate; trace Fibre; 2 g Protein; 48 mg Sodium

Paré Pointer

*Saved from hanging at the last minute, the crook said,
"No noose is good noose."*

Peachberry Clafouti

Vanilla custard topped with sweet peaches and blueberries. Serve it warm from a pretty baking dish for a nice ending to a meal, or serve it chilled.

Butter (or hard margarine), melted	1 tbsp.	15 mL
Large eggs	3	3
Milk	1 1/4 cups	300 mL
All-purpose flour	2/3 cup	150 mL
Granulated sugar	1/2 cup	125 mL
Vanilla extract	2 tsp.	10 mL
Grated lemon zest	1/2 tsp.	2 mL
Salt	1/8 tsp.	0.5 mL
Can of sliced peaches in juice, drained and chopped	14 oz.	398 mL
Frozen blueberries, thawed	1 cup	250 mL
Icing (confectioner's) sugar	1 tbsp.	15 mL

Whipped cream, for garnish
Fresh blueberries, for garnish
Fresh mint, for garnish

Brush 9 inch (23 cm) deep dish pie plate with butter.

Beat next 7 ingredients until smooth. Pour 1/2 cup (125 mL) into pie plate. Bake in 350°F (175°C) oven for about 6 minutes until mixture starts to set. Remove from oven.

Scatter peaches and blueberries over top. Pour remaining milk mixture over peach mixture. Bake for about 45 minutes until knife inserted in centre of custard comes out clean. Let stand on wire rack for 15 minutes.

Sprinkle with icing sugar.

Garnish with whipped cream, blueberries and mint. Serves 8.

1 serving: 178 Calories; 3.5 g Total Fat (1.0 g Mono, 0 g Poly, 1.5 g Sat); 57 mg Cholesterol; 32 g Carbohydrate; 2 g Fibre; 5 g Protein; 85 mg Sodium

Pictured on page 144.

Spiced Coconut Rice Pudding

A creamy and comforting rice pudding that's nicely spiced, with chewy toasted coconut for added flavour. Leftovers are great served cold, but can easily be reheated in the microwave.

Can of coconut milk	14 oz.	398 mL
Milk	1 1/2 cups	375 mL
Grated peeled cooking apple (such as McIntosh)	1/2 cup	125 mL
Short-grain white rice	1/2 cup	125 mL
Brown sugar, packed	1/4 cup	60 mL
Dark (navy) rum	1/4 cup	60 mL
Flaked coconut, toasted (see Tip, page 86)	1/4 cup	60 mL
Butter (or hard margarine), melted	1 tbsp.	15 mL
Vanilla extract	1 tsp.	5 mL
Grated lime zest	1/2 tsp.	2 mL
Ground cinnamon	1/4 tsp.	1 mL
Ground allspice	1/8 tsp.	0.5 mL
Salt	1/8 tsp.	0.5 mL

Combine all 13 ingredients in medium bowl. Transfer to greased 2 quart (2 L) casserole. Bake, covered, in 325°F (160°C) oven for about 90 minutes, stirring every 30 minutes, until rice is tender. Makes about 4 cups (1 L).

1 cup (250 mL): 483 Calories; 27.0 g Total Fat (2.0 g Mono, 0 g Poly, 23.0 g Sat); 11 mg Cholesterol; 47 g Carbohydrate; 1 g Fibre; 8 g Protein; 160 mg Sodium

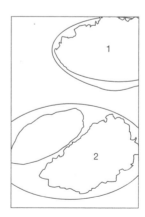

1. Dutch-Style Potato Bake, page 136
2. Cheesy Bruschetta Zucchini, page 138

Almond Peach Pudding

A soft and sweet pudding with pretty peaches and crunchy almonds—delightful topped with a dollop of whipped cream. Reheat leftover portions in the microwave for a quick and convenient treat.

Large eggs	4	4
Milk	2 cups	500 mL
Granulated sugar	1/4 cup	60 mL
Almond extract	1/2 tsp.	2 mL
Ground cinnamon	1/4 tsp.	1 mL
Ground nutmeg	1/8 tsp.	0.5 mL
Cans of sliced peaches in juice (14 oz., 398 mL, each), drained and halved	2	2
Frozen pound cake, thawed and cut into 3/4 inch (2 cm) cubes	10 1/2 oz.	298 g
Slivered almonds, toasted (see Tip, page 86)	1/3 cup	75 mL

Whisk first 6 ingredients in large bowl.

Add peaches and cake cubes. Stir until coated. Transfer to greased 9 x 13 inch (23 x 33 cm) baking dish.

Scatter almonds over top. Bake in 350°F (175°C) oven for about 50 minutes until knife inserted in centre comes out clean. Serves 10.

1 serving: 260 Calories; 10.0 g Total Fat (2.5 g Mono, 0.5 g Poly, 4.5 g Sat); 123 mg Cholesterol; 35 g Carbohydrate; 1 g Fibre; 7 g Protein; 181 mg Sodium

Pictured at left.

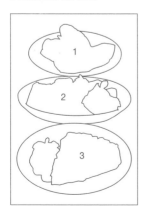

1. Chocolate Banana Crepes, page 146
2. Almond Peach Pudding, above
3. Peachberry Clafouti, page 141

Chocolate Banana Crepes

These delicious crepes can be assembled up to the point of baking and then chilled, covered, until you're ready to bake them.

All-purpose flour	1 cup	250 mL
Granulated sugar	2 tbsp.	30 mL
Ground cinnamon	1/4 tsp.	1 mL
Salt, just a pinch		
Large eggs	3	3
Milk	1 1/4 cups	300 mL
Butter (or hard margarine), melted	1 tbsp.	15 mL
Cooking oil	1 tbsp.	15 mL
Chocolate hazelnut spread	3/4 cup	175 mL
Medium bananas, halved lengthwise and crosswise	3	3
Chocolate hazelnut spread	1/4 cup	60 mL
Milk	1 tbsp.	15 mL
Hazelnut liqueur (or milk)	2 tsp.	10 mL
Chopped flaked hazelnuts (filberts), toasted (see Tip, page 86)	1/4 cup	60 mL

Combine first 4 ingredients in medium bowl. Make a well in centre.

Whisk next 3 ingredients in small bowl. Add to well. Whisk until smooth. Let stand for 1 hour.

Heat 1/4 tsp. (1 mL) cooking oil in small non-stick frying pan on medium. Stir batter. Pour about 3 tbsp. (50 mL) batter into pan. Immediately tilt and swirl pan to ensure bottom is covered. Cook for 1 to 2 minutes until top is set and brown spots appear on bottom. Turn crepe over. Cook for 30 seconds. Transfer to plate. Repeat with remaining cooking oil and batter. Makes about 12 crepes.

Spoon about 1 tbsp. (15 mL) of first amount of chocolate hazelnut spread along centre of each crepe. Arrange banana over top. Fold in sides. Fold up from bottom to enclose filling. Arrange, seam-side down, in greased 9 x 13 inch (23 x 33 cm) baking dish. Bake in 350°F (175°C) oven for about 10 minutes until heated through.

(continued on next page)

Combine second amount of chocolate hazelnut spread and milk in small microwave-safe bowl. Microwave, covered, on medium for 30 seconds (see Tip, page 21). Add liqueur. Stir until smooth. Drizzle over crepes.

Sprinkle with hazelnuts. Makes about 12 crepes.

1 crepe: 240 Calories; 11.0 g Total Fat (5.0 g Mono, 2.5 g Poly, 2.5 g Sat); 38 mg Cholesterol; 32 g Carbohydrate; 2 g Fibre; 5 g Protein; 45 mg Sodium

Pictured on page 144.

Mocha Bread Pudding

A deep, dark combination of rich chocolate and coffee in a moist bread pudding. Convert those that aren't fans of bread pudding by starting them out on a chocolate version!

Hot strong prepared coffee	1 1/2 cups	375 mL
Granulated sugar	1/2 cup	125 mL
Chocolate milk (see Note)	1 1/2 cups	375 mL
Vanilla extract	1 tsp.	5 mL
Large eggs	4	4
Salt	1/8 tsp.	0.5 mL
Day-old French bread slices (1/2 inch, 12 mm, thick), cut into 1 inch (2.5 cm) pieces	12	12
Dark chocolate bar, finely chopped	3 1/2 oz.	100 g

Stir coffee and sugar in medium bowl until sugar is dissolved.

Add chocolate milk and vanilla. Stir.

Whisk eggs and salt in large bowl. Slowly add milk mixture, whisking constantly until combined.

Add bread pieces and chocolate. Stir. Transfer to greased 2 quart (2 L) casserole. Let stand for 10 minutes. Bake, uncovered, in 325°F (160°C) oven for about 50 minutes until knife inserted in centre of pudding comes out clean. Let stand on wire rack for 15 minutes. Serves 8.

1 serving: 263 Calories; 7.0 g Total Fat (1.5 g Mono, 0.5 g Poly, 3.5 g Sat); 72 mg Cholesterol; 43 g Carbohydrate; 2 g Fibre; 7 g Protein; 300 mg Sodium

Strawberry Rhubarb Bake

A meringue-topped dessert with a buttery nut crust and a sweet fruity filling—perfect to enjoy after Sunday dinner. Try it chilled or at room temperature.

Butter (or hard margarine), softened	1 cup	250 mL
Granulated sugar	1 tbsp.	15 mL
All-purpose flour	2 cups	500 mL
Finely chopped pecans, toasted (see Tip, page 86)	1/4 cup	60 mL
Egg yolks (large)	6	6
Granulated sugar	2 cups	500 mL
Evaporated milk (or half-and-half cream)	1 cup	250 mL
All-purpose flour	1/4 cup	60 mL
Salt	1/4 tsp.	1 mL
Chopped fresh (or frozen, thawed) rhubarb	4 cups	1 L
Chopped fresh (or frozen, thawed) strawberries	2 cups	500 mL
Egg whites (large), see Safety Tip	6	6
Vanilla extract	2 tsp.	10 mL
Cream of tartar	1/2 tsp.	2 mL
Granulated sugar	2 tbsp.	30 mL

Beat butter and first amount of sugar in medium bowl until light and fluffy.

Combine first amount of flour and pecans in small bowl. Add to butter mixture, in 2 additions, stirring well until no dry flour remains. Press firmly into greased 9 x 13 inch (23 x 33 cm) baking dish. Bake in 350°F (175°C) oven for about 20 minutes until edges are golden.

Whisk next 5 ingredients in large bowl.

Add rhubarb and strawberries. Stir. Pour over bottom layer. Bake for about 65 minutes until knife inserted in centre of custard comes out clean.

Beat next 3 ingredients in separate medium bowl for about 3 minutes until soft peaks form.

(continued on next page)

Add sugar, 1 tbsp. (15 mL) at a time, beating constantly, until stiff peaks form and sugar is dissolved. Spread over second layer, making sure to seal completely. Bake for about 10 minutes until golden. Let stand in pan on wire rack until cool. Cuts into 18 pieces.

1 piece: 302 Calories; 14.0 g Total Fat (4.0 g Mono, 1.0 g Poly, 8.0 g Sat); 77 mg Cholesterol; 41 g Carbohydrate; 2 g Fibre; 5 g Protein; 130 mg Sodium

Safety Tip: This recipe contains uncooked egg. Make sure to use fresh, clean Grade A eggs that are free of cracks. Keep chilled and consume the same day the recipe is prepared. Always discard leftovers. Pregnant women, young children and the elderly are not advised to eat anything containing raw egg.

Pear Mango Crisp

A less-conventional fruit pairing creates the sweet filling of this classic oven-baked dessert, topped with a golden oat crust.

Chopped peeled pear	3 cups	750 mL
Chopped ripe (or frozen, thawed) mango	3 cups	750 mL
Brown sugar, packed	3 tbsp.	50 mL
Lime juice	1 tbsp.	15 mL
Cornstarch	2 tsp.	10 mL
Ground cinnamon	1/4 tsp.	1 mL
Ground cardamom	1/8 tsp.	0.5 mL
All-purpose flour	3/4 cup	175 mL
Brown sugar, packed	3/4 cup	175 mL
Quick-cooking rolled oats	3/4 cup	175 mL
Butter (or hard margarine), melted	1/3 cup	75 mL
Grated lime zest (see Tip, page 150)	1/2 tsp.	2 mL
Salt	1/8 tsp.	0.5 mL

Combine first 7 ingredients in large bowl. Transfer to greased 8 x 8 inch (20 x 20 cm) baking dish.

Combine remaining 6 ingredients in medium bowl. Sprinkle over pear mixture. Bake in 375°F (190°C) oven for about 35 minutes until filling is bubbling and topping is golden. Serves 8.

1 serving: 312 Calories; 8.0 g Total Fat (2.0 g Mono, 0.5 g Poly, 4.5 g Sat); 19 mg Cholesterol; 60 g Carbohydrate; 4 g Fibre; 3 g Protein; 94 mg Sodium

Blueberry Lemon Cornmeal Cake

Serve this pleasantly sweet cornmeal cake with tart bites of blueberry after dinner with coffee or tea. Reheat leftovers in the microwave for just-baked freshness.

Fresh (or frozen, thawed) blueberries	1 cup	250 mL
Granulated sugar	2 tbsp.	30 mL
Lemon juice	1 tbsp.	15 mL
Grated lemon zest (see Tip, below)	1/2 tsp.	2 mL
All-purpose flour	1 1/2 cups	375 mL
Yellow cornmeal	1 cup	250 mL
Granulated sugar	2/3 cup	150 mL
Baking powder	2 tsp.	10 mL
Baking soda	1 tsp.	5 mL
Salt	1/2 tsp.	2 mL
Large egg	1	1
Buttermilk (or soured milk, see Tip, page 94)	1 cup	250 mL
Butter (or hard margarine), melted	1/4 cup	60 mL
Icing (confectioner's) sugar	1 tbsp.	15 mL

Combine first 4 ingredients in medium bowl.

Combine next 6 ingredients in large bowl. Make a well in centre.

Whisk next 3 ingredients in small bowl. Add to well. Stir until just moistened. Spread about 2 1/2 cups (625 mL) in greased 9 x 9 inch (23 x 23 cm) pan. Scatter blueberry mixture over top. Drop remaining batter by mounded tablespoonfuls over blueberry mixture. Bake in 350°F (175°C) oven for about 35 minutes until wooden pick inserted in centre comes out clean. Let stand in pan on wire rack for 20 minutes.

Sprinkle with icing sugar. Cuts into 9 squares.

1 square: 290 Calories; 6.0 g Total Fat (1.5 g Mono, 0 g Poly, 3.5 g Sat); 31 mg Cholesterol; 53 g Carbohydrate; 1 g Fibre; 5 g Protein; 319 mg Sodium

 tip   When a recipe calls for grated zest and juice, it's easier to grate the fruit first, then juice it. Be careful not to grate down to the pith (white part of the peel), which is bitter and best avoided.

Maple Walnut Baked Alaska

Baked Alaska is a fun and old-fashioned favourite. This version has pound cake, maple walnut ice cream and a sweet meringue topping. Try it with your favourite ice cream for a personalized touch! This must be made in advance.

Frozen pound cake (10 1/2 oz., 298 g), thawed and cut into 1/2 inch (12 mm) slices	1/2	1/2
Maple walnut ice cream, softened	4 cups	1 L
Egg whites (large), see Safety Tip	5	5
Vanilla extract	1 tsp.	5 mL
Cream of tartar	1/2 tsp.	2 mL
Granulated sugar	1/3 cup	75 mL

Arrange cake slices in single layer in 9 inch (23 cm) deep dish pie plate, trimming to fit if necessary.

Pack ice cream into small plastic wrap-lined bowl. Smooth top. Invert ice cream onto cake slices. Freeze, covered, for at least 6 hours or overnight.

Beat next 3 ingredients in medium bowl for about 3 minutes until soft peaks form.

Add sugar, 1 tbsp. (15 mL) at a time, beating constantly, until stiff peaks form and sugar is dissolved. Spread over cake and ice cream, making sure to seal completely. Transfer to large baking sheet with sides. Bake on centre rack in 425°F (220°C) oven for about 6 minutes until golden. Serve immediately. Cuts into 8 wedges.

1 wedge: 284 Calories; 12.0 g Total Fat (1.0 g Mono, 0 g Poly, 7.0 g Sat); 66 mg Cholesterol; 39 g Carbohydrate; 0 g Fibre; 6 g Protein; 182 mg Sodium

Safety Tip: This recipe contains uncooked egg. Make sure to use fresh, clean Grade A eggs that are free of cracks. Keep chilled and consume the same day the recipe is prepared. Always discard leftovers. Pregnant women, young children and the elderly are not advised to eat anything containing raw egg.

Paré Pointer

That pig is a knight—his name is "Sir Lunchalot."

Measurement Tables

Throughout this book measurements are given in Conventional and Metric measure. To compensate for differences between the two measurements due to rounding, a full metric measure is not always used. The cup used is the standard 8 fluid ounce. Temperature is given in degrees Fahrenheit and Celsius. Baking pan measurements are in inches and centimetres as well as quarts and litres. An exact metric conversion is given below as well as the working equivalent (Metric Standard Measure).

Spoons

Conventional Measure	Metric Exact Conversion Millilitre (mL)	Metric Standard Measure Millilitre (mL)
1/8 teaspoon (tsp.)	0.6 mL	0.5 mL
1/4 teaspoon (tsp.)	1.2 mL	1 mL
1/2 teaspoon (tsp.)	2.4 mL	2 mL
1 teaspoon (tsp.)	4.7 mL	5 mL
2 teaspoons (tsp.)	9.4 mL	10 mL
1 tablespoon (tbsp.)	14.2 mL	15 mL

Cups

Conventional Measure	Metric Exact Conversion Millilitre (mL)	Metric Standard Measure Millilitre (mL)
1/4 cup (4 tbsp.)	56.8 mL	60 mL
1/3 cup (5 1/3 tbsp.)	75.6 mL	75 mL
1/2 cup (8 tbsp.)	113.7 mL	125 mL
2/3 cup (10 2/3 tbsp.)	151.2 mL	150 mL
3/4 cup (12 tbsp.)	170.5 mL	175 mL
1 cup (16 tbsp.)	227.3 mL	250 mL
4 1/2 cups	1022.9 mL	1000 mL (1 L)

Oven Temperatures

Fahrenheit (°F)	Celsius (°C)
175°	80°
200°	95°
225°	110°
250°	120°
275°	140°
300°	150°
325°	160°
350°	175°
375°	190°
400°	205°
425°	220°
450°	230°
475°	240°
500°	260°

Dry Measurements

Conventional Measure Ounces (oz.)	Metric Exact Conversion Grams (g)	Metric Standard Measure Grams (g)
1 oz.	28.3 g	28 g
2 oz.	56.7 g	57 g
3 oz.	85.0 g	85 g
4 oz.	113.4 g	125 g
5 oz.	141.7 g	140 g
6 oz.	170.1 g	170 g
7 oz.	198.4 g	200 g
8 oz.	226.8 g	250 g
16 oz.	453.6 g	500 g
32 oz.	907.2 g	1000 g (1 kg)

Pans

Conventional Inches	Metric Centimetres
8x8 inch	20x20 cm
9x9 inch	22x22 cm
9x13 inch	22x33 cm
10x15 inch	25x38 cm
11x17 inch	28x43 cm
8x2 inch round	20x5 cm
9x2 inch round	22x5 cm
10x4 1/2 inch tube	25x11 cm
8x4x3 inch loaf	20x10x7.5 cm
9x5x3 inch loaf	22x12.5x7.5 cm

Casseroles

CANADA & BRITAIN Standard Size Casserole	Exact Metric Measure	UNITED STATES Standard Size Casserole	Exact Metric Measure
1 qt. (5 cups)	1.13 L	1 qt. (4 cups)	900 mL
1 1/2 qts. (7 1/2 cups)	1.69 L	1 1/2 qts. (6 cups)	1.35 L
2 qts. (10 cups)	2.25 L	2 qts. (8 cups)	1.8 L
2 1/2 qts. (12 1/2 cups)	2.81 L	2 1/2 qts. (10 cups)	2.25 L
3 qts. (15 cups)	3.38 L	3 qts. (12 cups)	2.7 L
4 qts. (20 cups)	4.5 L	4 qts. (16 cups)	3.6 L
5 qts. (25 cups)	5.63 L	5 qts. (20 cups)	4.5 L

Recipe Index

153

154

155

156

157

If you like what we've done with **cooking**, you'll **love** what we do with **crafts**!